The Health Information Technology Dictionary

Richard Rognehaugh
Vice President, Chief Information Officer
Unity Health System
(Daughters of Charity National Health System)

AN ASPEN PUBLICATION®
Aspen Publishers, Inc.
Gaithersburg, Maryland
1999

Library of Congress Cataloging-in-Publication Data

Rognehaugh, Richard.
The health information technology dictionary/
Richard Rognehaugh.
p. cm.
ISBN 0-8342-1277-3 (alk. paper)
1. Medical informatics—Dictionaries.
2. Information technology—Dictionaries.
3. Information resource management—Dictionaries.
I. Title
R858.R64   1999
610'.1'4—dc21
98-46547
CIP

Orders: (800) 638-8437
Customer Service: (800) 234-1660

About Aspen Publishers • For more than 35 years, Aspen has been a leading professional publisher in a variety of disciplines. Aspen's vast information resources are available in both print and electronic formats. We are committed to providing the highest quality information available in the most appropriate format for our customers. Visit Aspen's Internet site for more information resources, directories, articles, and a searchable version of Aspen's full catalog, including the most recent publications: http://www.aspenpublishers.com
Aspen Publishers, Inc. • The hallmark of quality in publishing
Member of the worldwide Wolters Kluwer group.

Editorial Services: Nora Fitzpatrick
Library of Congress Catalog Card Number: 98-46547
ISBN: 0-8342-1277-3

Printed in the United States of America

2 3 4 5

PREFACE

The goal of providing this dictionary is to communicate health care information systems vocabulary within a common framework for better understanding. The intended audience of *The Health Information Technology Dictionary* is remarkably diverse. This resource addresses terms used by people and organizations across the health industry, including health information systems professionals, executive leaders, providers of health care, HMOs, PPOs, physicians, nurses, vendors, programmers, consultants, and patients.

The areas of marketplace application range from the private, public, state, and federal sectors: commercial insurers, Medicare and HCFA, Medicaid, and the Department of Defense (DoD) TRICARE.

Our goal is to provide the Gold Standard in comprehensive and evolving terms for this industry. We will attempt to republish upcoming editions in order to meet your future needs, and we solicit your feedback to further improve the outcome, for the benefit of people within the daily practice of health care information systems, and ultimately, for our patients.

ACKNOWLEDGMENTS

The creation of this book's content was aided immeasurably through the generous contribution of two talented experts. Susan E. Hughes is a career health care information executive and information systems officer, and Bruce Faraglia is an allied technology professional with significant applied work for the health information industry. I thank them both for their creative assistance and selfless dedication.

Richard Rognehaugh
Vice President, Chief Information Officer
Unity Health System
(Daughters of Charity National Health System)

10.0.0.0—private class A network available for intranet use; nodes with a 10.0.0.0 network address cannot communicate on the Internet, and the packets are not routed outside an autonomous system; *see also Class A*

127.0.0.1—loopback IP address; reserved IP address for node connectivity loopback testing; an affirmative response when pinging 127.0.0.1 indicates node Internet connectivity; *see also IP address, and PING*

802.3—*see IEEE 802.3*

80286—Intel microprocessor developed in 1984; employs a 16-bit internal and 16-bit external bus; used in IBM PC AT and clone computers and operates at speeds up to 12 MHz; capable of 3 MIPS; *see also MIPS*

80386DX—Intel microprocessor that employs a 32-bit internal and 32-bit external bus; operates at speeds up to 33 MHz; capable of 11 MIPS

80386SX—Intel microprocessor that employs a 32-bit internal and 16-bit external bus; operates at speeds up to 25 MHz; capable of 11 MIPS

80486DX—Intel microprocessor that employs a 32-bit internal and 32-bit external bus; operates at speeds up to 50 MHz; capable of 41 MIPS

80486DX2—Intel microprocessor that employs a 32-bit internal and 32-bit external bus; operates at speeds up to 66 MHz; capable of 41 MIPS

80486DX4—Intel microprocessor that employs a 32-bit internal and 32-bit external bus; operates at speeds up to 100 MHz; capable of 41 MIPS; the fastest 80486

80486SX—Intel microprocessor that employs a 32-bit internal and 32-bit external bus; operates at speeds up to 25 MHz; capable of 41 MIPS; an 80486 with the floating point unit disabled

80486SX2—Intel microprocessor that employs a 32-bit internal and 32-bit external bus; operates at speeds up to 50 MHz; capable of 41 MIPS

8086—Intel microprocessor developed in 1978; employs a 16-bit internal bus and 8-bit external bus; used in IBM PS/2 computers and operated at speeds up to 10 MHz; capable of 0.33 MIPS

8088—Intel microprocessor developed in 1978; employs an 8-bit internal bus and 8-bit external bus; used in IBM PC XT and clone computers and operated at speeds up to 10 MHz; capable of 0.33 MIPS

100BaseFX—Fast Ethernet over two-strand fiber optic cable; provides 100 Mbps baseband network capability up to four kilometers in length

100BaseT—Fast Ethernet or twisted pair Fast Ethernet; provides 100 Mbps baseband capability up to 100 meters in length

100BaseT4—Fast Ethernet or 4-pair category 3, 4, or 5 UTP or STP Fast Ethernet; provides 100 Mbps baseband capability up to 100 meters in length

100BaseTX—Fast Ethernet or 2-pair category 5 UTP or STP Fast Ethernet; provides 100 Mbps baseband capability up to 100 meters in length

100 Mbps—speed of a Fast Ethernet or FDDI network

10Base2—thinnet or thin Ethernet; provides 10 Mbps baseband network capability up to 185 meters in length; Ethernet network that employs a thin flexible coaxial cable for network node connectivity

10Base5—also called thicknet or thick Ethernet; provides 10 Mbps baseband network capability up to 500 meters in length

10BaseFL—Fiber Link Ethernet over fiber; provides 10 Mbps baseband network capability up to 2000 meters in length

10BaseT—the most common networking method in use today; known as Ethernet or twisted-pair Ethernet; provides 10 Mbps baseband network capability up to 100 meters in length

10 Mbps—10 million bits per second, speed of an Ethernet network

155 Mbps—speed of an ATM network

1Base5—provides 1 Mbps network capability over UTP up to 250 meters in length

3.5-inch disk drive—floppy storage drive capable of 720 KB, 1.44 MB or 2.88 MB of storage capacity

4GL—fourth-generation language; a category of computer programming languages that uses English-like, nonprocedural languages to achieve the computer program; in health care decision-support systems development, it can be used to design prototypes or products

5.25-inch disk drive—floppy storage drive capable of 360 KB or 1.2 MB of storage capacity; this type of floppy drive is no longer supported by Windows NT operating systems

8-inch disk drive—floppy storage drive produced by Remex and Shugart for use with CP/M; capable of 270 KB of storage in IBM, CP/M, and DEC formats

ACC—attendant console controller

access—providing a person the opportunity to approach, inspect, review, or make use of data or information; the communication between host and terminal

access control—a policy to determine who can have access to what data or information, or policies and procedures preventing access by those who are not authorized to have it; also, a process that specifies which data elements can be read, written, or erased by certain users of a system

access level—a level associated with an individual who may be accessing information (e.g., a clearance level) or with the information which may be accessed (e.g., a classification level); the authorized level at which an individual may access data, information, or computer systems

access measures—information that indicates how easy it is for a patient to gain access to medical services, including indicators of timeliness of care, annual turnover of Primary Care Providers (PCPs), patient choice of at least two PCPs, waiting time for urgent care and routine visits, timeliness of test results to patient and physician, availability of physicians and other caregivers, and geographical convenience; one of the key quality indicators for treating disease

access mode—an operation recognized by protection mechanisms as a possible operation on data or information; "read" and "write" are possible modes of access to a computer file; "execute" is a mode of access to a program; and "create" and "delete" are access modes for objects in a directory

access rights—the permissions that define a user's access to a computer network, a specific network server, or the files and directories located on a network server; access rights are assigned by department managers, supervisors, or network administrators, depending on the management structure

accidental threat—the threat of unintentional damage to a computer system and its data as a result of incorrect use of the system or natural phenomena, such as flood or fire

accountability—the concept that a person can be held responsible for certain actions, such as obtaining informed consent or disclosing confidential information; links all of the activities on the network to the user's identity; established procedures through which data security violations, or attempted violations, may be detected and traced to individuals who may then be held responsible

accountability information—a set of records, such as an audit trail, that provides documented evidence of the processing related to the security of the computer-stored confidential data

accuracy—magnitude of errors in data resulting from miscoding or misrepresenting facts, maintaining out-of-date findings, or commingling of data from more than one person; guarding against errors and unauthorized modifications

ACD—automatic call distribution; a feature of telecommunication systems that allows the ability to pass calls to the intended recipient without the need for human operators or receptionists

ACM—Association for Computing Machinery; founded in 1947 by John Mauchly and based in New York; a professional organization for those who work in various fields of information technology; currently has over 90,000 members worldwide

active intrusion—masquerading; trap doors; infiltration; piggybacking; *see browsing*

active star topology network—a network with a hub device that regenerates and repeats signals; the hub may contain diagnostic features that indicate faulty ports or that report fault information back to a management station; *see passive star topology network*

active star topology—a star-shaped network configuration with active hubs; active hubs regenerate and repeat signals; *see hub*

active threat—a potential breach of security that would cause actual damage or alteration to hardware, software, or data

activities—all care work ordered and/or performed on behalf of the patient; activities include nursing care, observation, consultations, investigations, tests, procedures, therapies, treatments, surgery, preventive care, and screening; the goal of health care activities is to improve health status

address class—one of four TCP/IP network types: Class A, B, C, or D; only A, B, and C are used in association with IP addressing; this electronic version of post office address uses number ranges to establish a solution to direct traffic to the proper location and devices which contain the corresponding address; ranges include Class A 1-126, Class B 128-191, Class C 192-223; *see class A, class B, class C*

Address Resolution Protocol—*see ARP*

administrative health care data—data collected that are unrelated to the status of the individual's health or health care; they include demographics, provider identification, caregiver identification, date and time of care, and other such data

administrative users access level—the special permission given to the team of users who maintain and support a network

administrator—a user with logon identification information who maintains system operations and tunes the system; also known as the admin, sysadmin, sysop, site admin, or site manager

advanced diagnostic card—a card used to run diagnostic checks on telephony cards and in automatic facilities test systems for testing trunk lines

advanced diagnostic card—*see ADC*

advanced organizational technologies—these include electronic data interchange systems, interactive video kiosks, and automated customer-response systems

Advanced Research Projects Agency of DoD—*see ARPA*

Advanced Research Projects Agency of DoD Network—*see ARPANET*

advanced RISC computing—*see ARC*

Advanced Technology—*see AT*

AG—application generator; software package such as Excel and LOTUS 1-2-3 that professionals may use to develop their own Health Decision Support System (HDSS) applications; *see HDSS*

AHIMA—American Health Information Management Association

AI—artificial intelligence; an output that exhibits behaviors associated with human intelligence

AIS privileges—automated information system permissions to access specified databases or perform specified functions within a computer system

algebraic cryptography—a process to encode text in which algebraic cipher replaces original plain text characters with numbers using a prearranged convention and then performs a reversible series of mathematical operations on the intermediate values

algorithm—a procedure for solving a mathematical problem in a specified number of steps that frequently involves repetition of an operation

ALOS—average length of stay; calculated as the average number of patient days of hospitalization for each admission, expressed as an average of the population within the plan for a given period of time

Alpha—DEC RISC 64-bit microprocessor

alphanumeric—data that consist of alphabetical characters and numbers or other special characters or symbols

ALU—arithmetic logic unit; portion of the CPU that performs the following arithmetic operations: addition, subtraction, multiplication, division, and negation

ambulatory care systems—another way of describing systems that provide assistance with either demand management, disease management, or wellness; *see also demand management, disease management, or wellness*

American National Standards Institute Organization—*see ANSI*

American Standard Code for Information Interchange—*see ASCII*

AMIA—American Medical Informatics Association

amplification techniques—formalization and quantification of heuristic judgment processes

amplifier—device used to increase the strength of broadband signals in order to travel further distances

analog data—data that are varied across a continuous range of values

analog signal—a continuous transmission signal that carries information in the form of varying waveforms/frequencies; may be voice or light signals; *see also digital*

analog-to-digital conversion—electrical conversion of analog signals to digital information

analytic representation—use of mathematical models or simulations of the environment requiring a decision

anchoring—the process by which specific and diverse parts of an image are segmented by graph readers to act as salient and relevant cues, or pointers, when extracting information

AND—logical gating operation that provides an output if all inputs are high

Anonymous FTP—Anonymous File Transfer Protocol; an FTP session that allows users to access designated public system resources (files); usually uses the logon name "anonymous" and password "guest"

ANSI—American National Standards Institute; founded in 1918, it oversees the development of electronics, data processing, and communications technology standards

answer device—a device configured to answer data calls; the device can be a data communications module connected to a computer or an outgoing modem

anti-tearing—the process or processes that prevent data loss when a smart card is withdrawn from the contacts during a data operation

API—application program interface; the messaging format and language that define how programs interact with functions in other programs, hardware drivers, or communications systems

APL—A Programming Language; a high-level language used for mathematical or scientific applications

AppleShare—a central file server and print server operating system that provides shared files and resources to AppleTalk users

AppleTalk—Apple Computer network protocol included free on every Macintosh computer; it is used on Apple networks in conjunction with LocalTalk, Ethernet, or token ring networks; implemented as a service in Windows NT to provide support for Macintosh file and print services

application—the use of information resources (information and information technology) to satisfy a specific set of user requirements; a program or set of programs that performs a task; the program used to direct the functions of a computer system

application generator—*see AG*

application layer—the application layer is seventh and highest layer of the Open Systems Interconnection, or OSI model that provides a path for the users' program to access the network through such various functions as remote file access, file transfer, directory services, and so on; the application layer passes program data and requests to the presentation layer; provides resources for the interaction that takes place between a user and application; *see OSI and presentation layer*

application metadata—data about a data dictionary concerning the structure and contents of forms, reports, and application menus

application program interface—*see API*

APR—adjusted payment rate; the amount of money that HCFA pays to risk contract HMOs; the figure is derived from the county AAPCC for the service area adjusted for the relative risks of the plan's enrollees; *see also AAPCC*

ARC—advanced RISC computing; used in the Windows NT boot loader to identify the path to the operating system; contains boot loader and operating system sections

architecture—a planned arrangement of components of a system

archiving—moving rarely or never accessed computer files to an off-line storage device, such as magnetic tape or optical disk system

ARCnet—Attached Resource Computer Network; 2.5 Mbps token-passing network architecture that employs a token (called an invitation)-passing network access scheme; can be used with twisted pair, coaxial cable, and fiber optics

arithmetic logic unit—*see ALU*

ARP—Address Resolution Protocol; used in TCP/IP networks to provide the physical address (MAC address) of a device from the assigned IP address

ARPA—Advanced Research Projects Agency of the Department of Defense; the government agency that funded the ARPANET

ARPANET—Advanced Research Projects Agency of the Department of Defense Network. TCP/IP packet-switched network developed by ARPA and used for network research from 1969 to 1990; consisted of approximately 150 sites that allowed resource sharing and remote login capability; was the precursor to the Internet as we know it today

artificial intelligence—*see AI*

ASCII—American Standard Code for Information Interchange; extensively used seven- or eight-bit standard information processing code that represents 128 standard characters used by PCs

ASO—administrative services only, typically a portion of the per-member per-month rate that is performed either by a payer or by a provider; a contract between an insurance company and a self-funded plan where the insurance company performs administrative services only and does not assume any risk; services usually include claims processing but may include other services, such as actuarial analysis, utilization review, etc.; *see also ERISA*

ASR—age/sex rate; the methodology used to develop health insurance premium pricing and group billing rates for various groupings of age and sex, using the applicable age/sex factors for a particular insurance product or group of patients; reflects the demographics of a group, rather than charging a premium for a single patient or family; *see also age/sex factor*

assignment of benefits—the payment of medical benefits directly to a provider of care rather than to a member; generally requires either a contract between the health plan and the provider or a written release from the subscriber to the provider allowing the provider to bill the health plan; the transfer of one's interest or policy benefits to another party

asymmetric multiprocessing—multiprocessing technique where certain tasks are dedicated to specific processors; one processor executes the operating system while another processor handles applications

asynchronous—a mode of data transmission that allows each character to be transmitted with its own start and stop bits to inform the receiving device of the beginning and end of a character

asynchronous communication—two-way communication in which there may be a time delay between the time a message is sent and the time it is received; *see also asynchronous*

asynchronous transfer mode—*see ATM*

AT—Advanced Technology; an early model series of IBM and clone computers using 80286 microprocessors that were known as AT computers

AT-Attachments—*see ATA*

ATA—AT-Attachments; an industry specification for the interfacing of hard disk drives to the PC/AT standard bus

ATM—asynchronous transfer mode; a connection oriented protocol that uses fixed 53-byte cells for information transmission; a packet-based communication protocol that provides the high bandwidth transmission rates required for multimedia communication; circuit-switched network ATM supports the simultaneous transmission of voice, video, and data and runs at OC-2 (155 Mbps), OC-3 (622 Mbps), and OC-4 (2.4 Gbps); *see also packet-switched network*

Attached Resource Computer Network—see ARCnet

attachment unit interface—*see AUI*

attack—the act of aggressively trying to bypass security controls in a computer system

attempted security violation—an unsuccessful action to gain unauthorized access to computer resources

attendant console controller—*see ACC*

attending physician—the physician responsible for the care and treatment of a patient in the hospital; a consulting physician or a physician employed by the hospital is not the attending physician

attribute—a piece of information describing a particular entity such as a file or directory

audio-teleconferencing—two-way electronic voice communications between two or more people at separate locations

audit, periodic—periodic audit is a repetitive procedure using a comprehensive checklist to assess requirements, vulnerabilities, procedures, responsibilities, certification criteria, and user problems for the purpose of making formal recommendations based on the findings

audit trail—documentary evidence of monitoring each activity of individuals on an information network; may be comprehensive or specific to the individual and information; for example, an audit trail may be a record of attempts to access a particularly sensitive file—electronic documentation of when and where a specific user gained access to the system and what changes the user made; used to track unauthorized access by authorized users, to determine if a security breach occurred and what, if anything, was lost during the breach

AUI—attached unit interface; connector port on network devices; also used for attachment to thick-wire, thicknet, Ethernet 10Base2 networks from networked stations

AUIC—attached unit interface cable; four twisted-pair cable wire that connects an Ethernet external transceiver to another Ethernet device

authenticate—to verify the identity of a user, user device, other entity, or the integrity of data stored, transmitted, or exposed to unauthorized modification in an information system

authentication—security measure, such as the use of digital signatures, to establish the validity of a transmission, message, or originator, or a means of verifying an individual's authorization to receive specific categories of information; the process of proving that a user or system is really who or what it claims to be—it protects against the fraudulent use of a system or the fraudulent transmission of information

authorization—mechanism for obtaining consent for the use and disclosure of personal information

authorized disclosure—granting of rights, which includes granting of access based on access rights; the release of personally identifiable information to a third party, such as an insurance carrier, upon authorization

autobaud detect—a data communications function that allows a data communications module to detect the baud rate of an incoming data transmission and automatically adjust to communicate at that rate

autocall—a data communication function that allows a computerized branch exchange to systematically place calls to a predetermined number

autocall number—an external telephone, data group, permanent telephone number, or temporary telephone number of a data line that the autocall feature uses

autocall override—a data communications function that allows a terminal user to call numbers other than the preset autocall number

autodial—a telecommunications function that allows simplified dialing of stored telephone numbers

automated planning and education system—an automated system to support management and end-user planning and education for information technology

automated utilization care plan—*see utilization care plan*

automatic call distribution—*see ACD*

automatic camp-on—a telecommunications functions that allows an incoming call party to automatically camp on to a busy station by remaining off hook; when the call encounters the busy signal, it is replaced by music, and when the desired extension is available the call is delivered

automatic queuing—a function that automatically puts a caller in a queue until a trunk becomes available for the connection to be made

autonomous processes—processes that provide active support to users by observing and tracking decision-making procedures to autonomously trigger appropriate responses

autonomous system—a collection of routers under single control using common IGP or RIP to pass routes back and forth to update route tables; *see also IGP and RIP*

auxiliary storage—*see secondary storage*

average cost per claim—a financial amount, representing the sum of the medical charge and administrative charge for services provided within the categories of admissions, physician services, and outpatient claims

average length of stay—*see ALOS*

average wholesale price—*see AWP*

AVGs—ambulatory visit groups; an outpatient classification scheme of 571 groupings

AWP—average wholesale price; the standard charge for a pharmacy item; derived by taking the average cost of the item to a pharmacy as charged by a large representation of pharmacy wholesale suppliers (for items not otherwise being sold at a discount)

back office function—generally refers to the administrative services, or some components of member services, physician services, accounting, and claims reimbursement, that must be performed in support of managed care contracting by either an insurer, MSO, PHO, or TPA; a managed care entity makes a determination of whether they are willing or able to perform these functions as an essential core business for a profit, or whether it is better to outsource the functions

back-propagation algorithm—a commonly used training algorithm to adjust weights in multilayer neural networks; the network is trained by back-propagating the error from output to hidden layer(s)

balance billing—the practice of a provider billing a patient for all charges not paid for by the insurance plan, because those charges are above the plan's UCR (usual, customary, and reasonable) or may be considered medically unnecessary; plans are increasingly prohibiting providers from balance billing except for allowed copays, coinsurance, and deductibles

bandwidth—the capacity of a communications device to carry information as measured by the difference between the highest and lowest frequencies that can be transmitted by that device

Banyan VINES—a networking operating system that allows users of PC desktop operating systems, such as OS/2, Windows, DOS, and Macintosh systems, to share information and resources with each other and with host computing systems; it allows organizations to build fully distributed computing environments around a suite of enterprise network services

bar code—form of technology in which identification data are coded into a series of bars; can be used on smart cards to identify the card carrier

baseband—the use of an entire bandwidth for digital bidirectional data transmission; only one transmission at a time is possible in baseband networks; an Ethernet network is a baseband for network based printers

baseline—compiled performance statistics for use in the planning and analysis of systems and networks

BASIC—Beginner's All-purpose Symbolic Instruction Code; a fairly simple programming language that uses a compiler to generate an operating object code program; BASIC was also included through the function keys on early IBM 8088 computers

Basic Input/Output System—*see BIOS*

batch—a group of claims for different patients from one office submitted in one computer transmission, or a group of claims processed by a claims processor

baud rate—the reference to transfer speed of a data communication system, defined in the number of symbols per second

bed days per 1000—*see days per thousand*

benchmarking—a process of comparing one's own health care practice or entity to the finest in the business, in order to improve the quality of care or services by constantly observing how the most efficient comparable organizations across the country are run; some accreditation organizations, such as the Joint Commission, have adopted Malcolm Baldridge formats and have made benchmarking an essential element for planning within health care organizations; *see also QI*

beneficiary—person or persons specified by a policyholder as eligible to receive insurance policy proceeds (private or government)

benefit—amount payable by the insurance company to a claimant, assignee, or beneficiary when the insured suffers a loss covered by the policy

benefit management—this module within a managed care information system must handle a minimum of: multiple plans, products, and levels within those respective plans and products; tracking defined benefits and events; and benefit limits by service or dollar

BGP—Border Gateway Protocol; used to advertise the networks that can be reached within an autonomous system; newer than the EGP (Exterior Gateway Protocol)

billed charge—see submitted charge; *see also FFS*

billed charges with maximum—the hospital and HMO agree that the HMO will pay billed charges, but a ceiling or cap is placed on charges, with the HMO responsible for all charges up to the cap

billed claims—see submitted charge; *see also FFS*

biometric—a unique personal characteristic, such as a signature, hand geometry, or fingerprint; a measurement of a physical feature or repeatable action of an individual (e.g., hand geometry, voice print, retinal scan, iris scan, fingerprint patterns, facial characteristics) that can be used to identify one person from another

BIOS—Basic Input/Output System; the first operating system code that executes upon computer boot-up; contained in flash memory or ROM firmware on the motherboard

bit—Binary digit; first termed by John Tukey in 1949 using the base 2 methodology, the smallest basic unit of electronic information associated with computers and information processing; sometimes a bit is considered to be either on or off, or an O or I value

bitmap—an image stored as a pattern of pixels corresponding bit by bit with the associated image; used by computers because of its simplicity

bit order—the transmission order of a serial transmission system

bits per second—*see bps*

blended capitation—a reimbursement mechanism which mixes some proportion of traditional fee-for-service with some proportion of AAPCC capitated reimbursement

block algorithms—formulas that encrypt data one block at a time

BNC—bayonet nut connector; T-connector or barrel connector used in conjunction with thin-wire, thinnet, coaxial cable, and Ethernet 10Base2 networks; used for connection between a networked station and the network (T-connector) and to extend the network (barrel connector)

booting—process of loading an operating system into a computer random access memory; *see also RAM*

BOOT.INI—Windows NT operating system boot process file with information on how a particular machine will boot; maintains information on boot operating systems and their locations on the hard drive; also provides boot-up menu boot options

boot partition—partition that contains the operating system files

BOOTP—BOOTstrap Protocol; a protocol that provides start up (boot) information to devices from a remote host; used with diskless workstations and hubs

BOOTSECT.DOS—Windows NT operating system boot process file that executes if an operating system other than Windows NT is selected through the boot-up menu

BOOTstrap Protocol—*see BOOTP*

Border Gateway Protocol—*see BGP*

bounce—an act of gracefully shutting down a system and subsequent restarting or rebooting of it; bouncing a system ensures system changes are active and problem areas are cleared due to the re-boot process; synonymous with UNIX systems

bound applications—programs compiled to run under DOS or OS/2

Bourne Shell—original and most widely used interactive command interpreter and programming language UNIX shell; prompted by $; introduced in 1978 and named after its creator, Steven Bourne

bps—bits per second; basic unit of speed associated with data transmission; *see also baud rate*

breach of confidentiality—breach of contract in which an individual reveals an entrusted confidence without the other person's consent

breach of security—any action by an authorized user that results in a negative impact upon the data in a system or the system itself, or that it causes data or services within a system to suffer unauthorized disclosure, modification, destruction, or denial of service

bridge—a computer or device that connects two similar local area networks (LAN) that use the same LAN protocols; bridges use the store and forward packetizing technique and operate at the data-link layer, second layer, of the OSI model

broadband—the use of all bands of overall bandwidth for unidirectional data transmission, in a frequency-modulated fashion over a segment of the total bandwidth available; multiple transmissions can occur at the same time in broadband networks

broadband network—the basic term for a computer network capable of high-bandwidth transmission; *see also ATM*

broad-band technology—*see broadband*

broadcast—a network transmission or packet delivery technique that sends and delivers a single message for all nodes on a network

broadcast storm—result of the number of broadcast messages on the network reaching or surpassing the bandwidth capability of the network

brouter—bridging router; a device that provides both bridging and routing functions; acts as a bridge for some protocols and a router for the rest; *see also bridge and router*

browser—a program or software tool that supports graphics and hyperlinks and is used to view data and examine the contents of a database or knowledge base, or to view other documents on the World Wide Web

browsing—legitimate access with browsing to obtain unauthorized information

budget—a financial plan identifying expected expenditures and revenues for a particular time period it identifies structures and allocates resources to provide some service or product over a specified period of time

buffer—temporary storage holding areas for input or output data mainly used to compensate for differences in data flows

bug—unwanted or unintended programming mistake or hardware error condition that causes system errors/malfunctions and unpredictable system actions; errors in computer code that cause a system to fail or work improperly

bus—the internal connector on a PC motherboard into which expansion boards are plugged

bus network—type of inexpensive LAN topology where networked nodes are connected to the main cable of the network; usually implemented where 10 or fewer users need a temporary network; employs CSMA/CD

byte—series of eight 0 or 1 bits used to represent a character, bytes are usually counted in kilobytes, megabytes, and gigabytes; first termed by Werner Buchholz in 1956

cable—an assembly of one or more insulated wires within a common protective sheath

cache—small area of temporary computer memory storage space that speeds data access for frequently accessed RAM locations

Cairo—Microsoft's original (code) name for the Windows NT 4.0 operating system

calendar errors—errors typically caused by the inability to handle the Year 2000 with four bytes versus the two-byte data fields of earlier systems, or by failing to treat it as a leap year and converting incorrectly between date representations

call screen transfer capability—allows a telephone call to be transferred, together with a visual set of data about the caller, therefore eliminating the need for asking the caller duplicate questions; a preferred customer service feature, which adds a caring perspective together with response-time efficiency; *see also integrated call management*

cap rate—*see capitation rate*

capitated payment—a contractually agreed fee (monthly, bimonthly, or annual) paid by an HMO or CMP to either an IDN, hospital, physician, or group practice in exchange for health care services to enrolled members

capitation rate—providers and HMOs (and other "customer-supplier" entities) negotiate a rate per enrollee, per time period (often monthly); the provider renders all contracted care and services to members for a prospective payment with retroactive adjustments, taking the risk that the capitation rate will be sufficient to cover all of the costs of care to members; similar agreements can be made between the hospital/delivery system and physician groups, for either primary care providers or specialists

card-dispensing machine—*see CDM*

card reader—equipment capable of reading the information on a smart card, such as that in the magnetic stripe or chip

carrier—a telecommunications company regulated by governmental agencies that offers communication relay services to the general public via shared circuits, charging published and non-discriminatory rates

Carrier Sense Multiple Access with Collision Detection—*see CSMA/CD*

Carrier Sense Multiple Access with Collision Avoidance—*see CSMA/CA*

CASE—computer-aided software engineering; a contemporary system development model that can assist by automating any or all of the system analysis and system design components in such a way as to organize, structure, and simplify the system development process

case-based reasoning—rather than using a set of rules, this type of reasoning draws from a library of similar cases, to assist in decision making; *see also expert system*

case management—*see CM*

case management module—*see case management system*

case management system—this module is a financial tracking tool for the cost of care on a per patient basis; it provides analysis and automated comparisons of the annual benefit limits to care plan projected costs to actual daily expenditures of labor and material resources on a per patient, per disease, or per payer basis

case-mix information—information grouped according to standards, such as diagnosis-related groups (DRGs), that integrate clinical and financial data; by identifying bundles of goods and services delivered to each patient, it is possible to predict and control the use of resources

case-mix information system—*see CMIS*

CAT-1—Category 1 unshielded twisted pair cable (UTP); allows voice grade–only transmission rates below 4 Mbps up to 100 meters or 328 feet in length per segment

CAT-2—Category 2 unshielded twisted pair cable (UTP); allows voice grade–only transmission rates below 4 Mbps up to 100 meters or 328 feet in length per segment

CAT-3—Category 3 unshielded twisted pair cable (UTP); allows a data transmission rate of 10 Mbps up to 100 meters or 328 feet in length per segment

CAT-4—Category 4 unshielded twisted pair cable (UTP); allows a data transmission rate of 16 Mbps up to 100 meters or 328 feet in length per segment

CAT-5—Category 5 unshielded twisted pair cable (UTP); allows a data transmission rate of 100 Mbps up to 100 meters or 328 feet in length per segment

Category 1 unshielded twisted pair cable (UTP)—*see CAT-1*

Category 2 unshielded twisted pair cable (UTP)—*see CAT-2*

Category 3 unshielded twisted pair cable (UTP)—*see CAT-3*

Category 4 unshielded twisted pair cable (UTP)—*see CAT-4*

Category 5 unshielded twisted pair cable (UTP)—*see CAT-5*

CDFS—CD-ROM File System; a 32-bit file system used in conjunction with CD-ROMs on Windows 95 and Windows NT machines

CCITT—Coordinating Committee on International Telephony and Telegraphy; a standards-setting body; organization that coordinates international internetworking research and development

CDM—card-dispensing machine; machine from which stored value cards may be purchased

CDR—clinical data repository; a structured, systematically collected storehouse of patient-specific clinical data; a component of the computer-based patient record

CD-ROM—compact disk read-only memory; read-only optical data storage device capable of 640 MB of storage; used for applications that require massive amounts of data storage and for multimedia; applications include imagine, reference, and large databases

CD-ROM File System—*see CDFS*

CDSS—clinical decision support system; a subclass of HDSSs that provides clinical data banks and algorithms, analytic or pathophysiologic models, clinical decision theoretical models, statistical pattern recognition methods, symbolic reasoning, and clinical expert knowledge bases to support and enhance diagnostic thinking and cognitive reasoning strategies of expert and nonexpert clinicians

cell—fixed-size 53-byte cell (packet) used on ATM networks; each cell contains 48 bytes of data and a 5-byte header

Central Processing Unit—*see CPU*

century date—another description for the Year 2000, and a system's ability to properly process the data field for a 4-byte year; *see also Y2K*

century date-compliant—*see Y2K compliant*

CERT—computer emergency response team

certificate revocation list (CRL)—a listing of public key certificates that have been revoked by a company's certification authority

certification—the administrative act of approving a system for use in a particular application

certification authority—a trusted issuer of certification

Certified NetWare Engineer—*see CNE*

Certified NetWare Administrator—*see CNA*

Certified NetWare Instructor—*see CNI*

CGA—color graphics adapter; the first IBM PC and compatible color display system providing 16 colors at a resolution of 160 x

100, four colors at a resolution of 320 x 200, and 2 colors at a resolution of 640 x 200

CGI—common gateway interface; a standard for running extended programs from a WWW server, which specifies how to pass arguments from the executing program as part of the HTTP request; *see also WWW and HTTP*

Challenge Handshake Authentication Protocol—*see CHAP*

channel—a telecommunications line or pathway for the transmission of signals between transmitting and receiving devices, such as a telephone or personal computer devices

Channel Service or Sharing Unit/Data Service Unit—*see CSU/DSU*

CHAP—Challenge Handshake Authentication Protocol; Windows NT password authentication method that uses the RSA Data Security MD5 (Message Digest Five) algorithm; used in conjunction with the remote access server (RAS) for dial-in connections to a Windows NT Server

check digit—the result of a checksum operation

checksum—digits or bits summed according to arbitrary rules and used to verify the integrity of data

Chicago—Microsoft's development code name for the Windows 95 operating system

chief information officer—*see CIO*

CHIN—community health information network; an electronic network to share medical information within a community of care entities, in a way that connects hospitals, clinics, rehab facilities, pharmacies, insurers, physicians, employers, and others having a need for the information; also called health information networks (HINs), regional health information networks (RHINs), enterprise information networks (EINs), and community health management information systems (CHMISs)

chip—a small piece of thin semiconductor material, such as silicon, that has been chemically processed to have a specific set of electrical characteristics, such as circuits, storage, and/or logic elements

chip card—a card containing an integrated circuit chip; it can be a microprocessor or a simple memory chip

chip (or card) operating system (COS)—a set of instructions permanently burned into the programmable read-only memory (PROM) of an integrated circuit chip (ICC) or built into the ICC during manufacture; the instructions usually constitute some primary security and memory management functions

CI—clinical integration; an approach to provide patient care with a coordination of comprehensive clinical services for individual persons and for populations

CIO—chief information officer; a top-level information system executive who is responsible for managing information systems, information technology, and the management of information within an organization

ciphertext—encrypted text that is unreadable

circuit switched network—a telecommunications network that connects parties by establishing a dedicated circuit between them

CIS—community information system; *see CHIN*

CISC—complex instruction set computer processor; CISC computers use microprocessors with large numbers of execution steps and many clock cycles to operate; Intel computers are CISC computers

claim—the bill for a patient by his or her provider for medical services that were provided, from which processing for payment to the provider or patient is made; a demand to the insurers by or on behalf of an insured person for the payment of benefits under a policy; an act or omission that the insured reasonably believes will result in an express demand for damages to which this insurance applies

claims processing and payment—this module with a health care information system must handle a variety of tasks, including: tracking of claims and payment to the authorization, benefits, eligibility, and premiums or capitations paid; matching diagnosis, procedure, location, service codes, etc.; capitation with allowance of fee-for-service patients for multiple models; calculation of payments and benefits; routine edits, such as duplicate payment, or age/sex; explanation of benefits; multiple risk or withhold options, Preferred Provider Organization processing, and third-party administrator fund management; and claim check payment capabilities

class—in object-oriented analysis and design, it represents a classification of objects that share common attributes; *see also object-oriented programming*

Class A—0-126 IP addressing scheme based on the first octet in the IP address; provides over 16 million hosts per network

Class B—128-191 IP addressing scheme based on the first octet in the IP address; provides up to 65,534 hosts per network

Class C—192-223 IP addressing scheme based on the first octet in the IP address; provides up to 254 hosts per network

classification level—the security level of information

clear—setting of a register or bit to zero

clearance level—the security level of an individual who may access information up to the authorized level

clear text—unencoded text that can easily be read; *see plain text*

client—computer that has access to a network and resources shared on that network and requests services from a server; the client computer does not store all the data or software it uses, but functions through the use of centralized network server data and/or software; *see also server*

client-server model— a computer network architecture that places frequently used information on centrally accessible server computers, which can be retrieved as it is needed across the network by client computers; this model splits the processing between clients and servers on a network by assigning functions to the machine most able to perform the function

client-server architecture—*see client-server model*

Client Services for NetWare—*see CSNW*

Clinger-Cohen Act of 1996—Information Technology Management Reform Act; Public Law 104-106

clinical algorithm—*see medical protocols*

clinical data—all relevant clinical and socioeconomic data disclosed by a patient and others, as well as observations, findings, therapeutic interventions and prognostic statements generated by the members of a health care team

clinical data information systems—automated systems that serve as a tool to inform clinicians about tests, procedures, and treatment in an effort to increase efficiency and decrease managed health care utilization, without losing quality of care; clinical systems are becoming the fastest growth segment of the information systems industry, replacing financial and patient accounting emphasis of the past

clinical data repository—collection of clinical data from diverse sources; supports monitoring and analysis of patient care outcomes; an automated data storage tool that acts as a warehouse for retrievable patient data that can be aggregated into reports or extracts to aid decision making; may be a component of an institutional information warehouse and/or a community or state health information system

clinical decision support system—*see CDSS*

clinical guideline—a set of steps to be taken in the management of a clinical condition

clinical information/data—information/data related to the health and health care of an individual collected from or about an individual receiving health care services; may include the provider's evaluation of a patient's physical or mental state of health; descriptions of an individual's health history or family health history; diagnostic studies; decision rationale; descriptions of procedures performed; findings; therapeutic interventions; medications prescribed; description of responses to treatment; prognostic statements; and descriptions of socioeconomic and environmental factors related to the patient's health

clinical integration—*see CI*

clinical outlier—cases that cannot adequately be assigned to an appropriate DRG owing to unique combinations of diagnoses and surgeries, very rare conditions, or other unique clinical reasons; such cases are grouped together into clinical outliers DRGs

clinical pathways—*see medical protocols*

clinical protocol—*see medical protocols*

clipper chip—a data encryption chip used by the federal government in data communications equipment, such as computers, modems, fax machines, and phones for protection from hackers, intruders, and criminals

clock speed—the speed at which a microprocessor or an expansion bus operates; the number of electronic pulses a microprocessor can produce each second; expressed in megahertz; *see also megahertz*

closed card system—a smart card system in which the cards can only be used in a specified environment, such as a college campus; *see open card system*

closed system—a system that does not share information with another system; the goal of supporting a closed system is to maintain the daily operation, viability, and changing requirements within this single system; *see also open systems architecture*

cluster—disk storage unit of 1024 bytes

CM—case management; a patient management process that is based on caseload information, including clinical assessment, coordinated placement of the patient into the appropriate medical setting, regular monitoring, and periodic evaluation and follow-up of the patient

CMIS—clinical management information system; an information system that supports and clinically integrates patient care, provides coordination of care for individual persons and for populations, and logically corresponds with vertical integration and the development of a continuum of care

C-MIS—case-mix information system; a system that accommodates case-mix data regarding the clinical and cost aspects of categories of patient mix; *see also case-mix information*

CMM—cumulative member months; an aggregate number used to quantify any given period of plan coverage representing the sum of the months multiplied by the members enrolled for each month

CNA—Certified NetWare Administrator; entry-level Novell certification; CNAs provide day-to-day resource administration on NetWare systems and install, upgrade, configure, and maintain applications while monitoring network performance and implementing security

CNE—Certified NetWare Engineer; introduced in 1989; intermediate-level Novell certification; CNEs provide implementation, tuning, integration, and networking engineering on multiple NetWare systems and specialize in NetWare3, NetWare 4, UnixWare, or GroupWare

CNI—Certified NetWare Instructor; advanced level Novell certification; CNIs teach NetWare concepts, installation, and configuration and are Novell technical resources

coaxial cable—a network/communications cable medium consisting of an inner conductor encased in a clear/white insulation and a braided outer conductor surrounded by black PVC insulation; RG-8 (thicknet), RG-11 (thicknet), RG-58 (thinnet), and RG-62 (ARCnet) are common network coaxial cable types

COB—coordination of benefits; based on policy guidance within the National Association of Insurance Commissioners (NAIC) to prevent double payment for services when an enrollee has coverage from two or more sources; for example, a husband may have Blue Cross and Blue Shield through work, and the wife may have elected an HMO through her job—the COB agreement gives the order for what organization has primary responsibility for payment; used to ensure that the insured's benefits from all sources do not exceed 100% of allowable

cohort data—a data set that follows individuals over time; data describe a specific group of people (cohort) who are defined by a common characteristic at a point in time and then followed

collision—the result of two nodes on a network attempting to use a shared network at the same time

collision detection—the ability of a transmitting node to detect traffic on an Ethernet (baseband) shared network; if a transmitting station detects silence it will transmit data—if a collision takes place, the transmitting station will wait a random amount of time before attempting to retransmit the entire message; *see CSMA/CD*

color graphics adapter—*see CGA*

COM—*see computer output to microfilm*

command interpreter—program that accesses and executes user input; the Bourne, C, and Korn shells are used with UNIX; COMMAND.COM is associated with DOS machines

comm closet—room or location where network electronic equipment resides and where drops terminate; also known as a wiring closet

Common Gateway Interface (CGI)—*see CGI*

Common Object Request Broker Architecture (CORBA)—architecture used in object-oriented models to provide message-passing communication between objects

communications architecture—the hardware and software infrastructure that implements the communications function

community information system—*see CIS*

community care network—*see CHIN*

compact disk-read only memory—*see CD-ROM*

compact flash smart card—a smart card that uses nonvolatile flash memory; when the computer is turned off, the data are not lost

compiled language—code that is compiled; all lines of code are translated one time into an executable file; runs fast

complete trust domain—Windows NT large complex network domain with multiple account and resource domains; two-way trusts are maintained to each and every domain; complete trust domains are not very common

complex instruction set computer processor—*see CISC*

compliant—used to define Year 2000, or century date-compliant hardware, software, or networks; a compliant system's year date can be stored and exchanged without being misinterpreted as the year 1900, 2100, or other invalid date; compliant systems have no extended semantics, calendar errors, date overflow, or inconsistent semantics

component-ware—application software that supports physician and patient information systems within a health "enterprise" by tying together multiple software objects that support departmental or functional processes; components may include laboratory, billing, referral trends, scheduling, or patient satisfaction functions

compression—compression of images through software is used to save storage or transmission space; compressed images used for diagnostic purposes must be loss less, while images used in consultation can be lossy; process executed through software to reduce file size for storage or transmission; Windows NT provides real-time, file-by-files, speed-over-size compression for storage; PPP employs compression when transferring data; modem also employs compression for data transmission; *see lossless compression, lossy compression, and PPP*

Computer Abuse—the commission of acts involving a computer, which may not be illegal but are unethical.

computer-aided software engineering—*see CASE*

computer-based patient record—*see CPR*

Computer-Based Patient Record Institute—*see CPRI*

computer-based patient record system—an entire system, supporting the CPR, that provides the functionality to support data capture, storage, processing communication, security, and presentation; it includes the people, data, rules and procedures, processing and storage devices, and communication and support facilities for the presentation of computer-based patient record information

computer crime—the commission of illegal acts committed through the use of a computer or against a computer system

computer emergency response team (CERT)—a team of system specialists and other professionals, such as lawyers, who investigate computer break-ins and attacks

computer network—a group of computers and peripheral devices, such as printers, that are physically and logically connected together to share information

computer output to microfilm—a method of long-term storage of computer files on microfilm

computer patient record—*see CPR*

computer security—technologic safeguards and administrative procedures applied to computer hardware, programs, and data to protect organizational assets and the privacy of individuals

concentrator—network device where networked nodes are connected; used to divide a data channel into two or more channels of lower bandwidth; *see hub*

concurrent review—a general method of identifying superfluous activities in health service delivery; concurrent review works by the regular measurement of health status, care activities, and management decisions, coupled with appropriate feedback of this information to the physicians and nurses who provided the care

confidential—information which is not freely disclosed; private information that is entrusted to another with the confidence that unauthorized disclosure, which would be prejudicial to the individual, will not occur

confidential health care information—information relating to a person's health care history, diagnosis, condition, treatment, or evaluation; any data or information, whether oral or recorded in any form or medium (paper, microfilm, or in computer-retrievable form), that identifies or can readily be associated with the identity of a patient, and relates to a patient's health care or is obtained in the course of a patient's health care

confidential information—information that is perceived by a person to be confidential and must be protected from unauthorized disclosure

confidentiality—the act of limiting disclosure or improper use of information without proper authorization and authentication; maintaining the trust that an individual has placed in another whom has been entrusted with private matters; the status accorded to data or information indicating that it is sensitive for some reason, and needs to be protected against theft or improper use and must be disseminated only to individuals or organizations authorized to have access to it

configuration management (CM)—in relation to hardware, CM may be a database that contains information about workstations, servers, bridges, routers, and other equipment on the network, such as type of equipment, model, etc.; in relation to software, CM provides a history, such as date of installation of the software, dates of changes to the software, version numbers, etc.

connectivity—the potential of a computer system to establish links to or interact with another computer system or database

consent—the agreement of an individual for a given action relative to that individual; in health care, consent refers to a communication process between the provider and the patient, and may refer to consent for treatment, special procedures, release of information, and advance directives

contact—an electrical connecting surface between an integrated circuit chip and its interfacing device that permits a flow of current

contingency plan—a plan for responding to the loss of a system due to a disaster, such as a flood, fire, computer virus, or major hardware or software failure; the plan contains procedures for emergency response, backup, and post-disaster recovery

continuing care—*see LTC*

controlled access—controlled access means that each authorized user is permitted access to data and resources within the data system according to that user's authorization, but to no more

controlled resource—a resource to which an access control mechanism has been specifically applied

control program for microcomputers—*see CP/M*

control rights—a person has the right to know where his or her data are stored, to know who can access his or her own data, to correct his or her own record, to make certain segments inaccessible via a standard process, and to ensure that the data keeper observes the tenets of laws and professional ethics

control unit—*see CU*

conventional memory—the 0-640 KB range of RAM used by MS-DOS to run real-mode applications

conversion—the process of making changes to databases or source code

cookies—chunks of information that are sent from web sites to an individual's Internet browser; the browsers save these cookies on the system's hard drive; cookies help the programs at the web site keep track of what the user has been doing during the "visit" at the web site—e.g., what you look at and where you go next

cooperative multitasking—processor multitasking operation that allows programs to interact with each other and control the processor; Win16 applications are cooperative multitasked applications in Windows NT and OS/2

Coordinating Committee on International Telephony and Telegraphy—*see CCITT*

CORBA—Common Object Request Broker Architecture

core memory—volatile data storage memory used in 1960s vintage computers; invented at MIT in 1952, it employed thousands of read, write, and clear wires running through metallic ferrite donuts that each stored one bit of data

CP/M—control program for microcomputers; operating system used on the 1970s vintage Zilog Z80 computers

CPR—computer-based patient record; electronically maintained information about an individual's lifetime health status and health care; it resides in a computer-based patient record system and is an electronic patient record that resides in a system specifically designed to make complete and accurate data, alerts, reminders, clinical decision support systems, links to medical knowledge, and other aids

CPRI—**Computer-based Patient Record Institute**—a non-profit membership organization, established in January 1992, to initiate and coordinate activities that promote the routine use of CPRs throughout health care; focuses on policy, evaluation, concepts, and standards

CPU—central processing unit; brain of the computer; main system board (motherboard) integrated chip that directs computer operations; performs the arithmetic, logic, and controls operations in the computer

crash—a data system error that leads to a total cessation of all computing activities and requires a restart procedure to recover the normal operational status

critical success factors—*see CSFs*

CRL—*see certificate revocation list*

crossover claim—a bill for services rendered to a patient receiving benefits simultaneously from Medicare and Medicaid, or other carriers, in which Medicare pays first and then determines the amounts of unmet Medicare deductible and coinsurance to be paid by Medicaid

crosstalk—signal overflow from one wire to an adjacent wire with the possibility of causing information distortion; UTP cable is the most susceptible transmission media to crosstalk

cryptography—the term covering the methods and processes of transforming an understandable form into an unintelligible form, and reconverting it back into the original form; the art of keeping data secret, primarily through the use of mathematical or logical functions that transform intelligible data into seemingly unintelligible data and back again; a collection of techniques for keeping information secure; method to transform written words and other kinds of messages so that they are unintelligible to unauthorized recipients; *see substitution, and transposition*

CSFs—critical success factors; factors that are most important for achieving business success, or success in the design and implementation of an information system

C Shell—interactive UNIX shell developed by William Joy and the University of California; prompted by % and features a C programming look and feel

CSMA/CA—carrier sense multiple access with collision avoidance; media access control protocol; technique used to avoid collisions on a network; allows multiple nodes to operate on a network by sending intent to transmit signal before the transmission of data; CSMA/CA is used on AppleTalk networks, and can save transmission time and bandwidth

CSMA/CD—carrier sense multiple access with collision detection; media access control protocol; technique used to avoid collisions on a network; allows multiple nodes to operate on a network by listening for traffic and the transmission of data when the network is idle or silent; CSMA/CD is used on Ethernet networks

CSNW—Client Services for NetWare; provides the ability to connect to and make a NetWare server's resources available to Windows NT workstation; implements the NWLink (Microsoft's implementation of IPX/SPX) network protocol when loaded

CSU/DSU—channel sharing unit/data service unit; a unit that shapes digital signals for transmission; often incorrectly identified as a modem

CU—control unit; portion of the CPU that coordinates all computer operations through the machine cycle: fetch, decode, execute, and store

CyberCash—protocol for sending secure payment instructions over the Internet

cyberspace—popular term now associated with the Internet, or the realm of communications and computation available on the Internet

cyberspace shadow—the model in cyberspace of a person or of an organization; e.g., a person's credit records, medical files, driving records, and criminal records

cycle time—used to describe the turnaround time (TAT) from start to finish for a particular process, such as claims processing

Cyclic Redundancy Checks (CRC)—a mathematical means to digitally fingerprint or perform an error check on a block of data

data—any discrete, uninterpreted observations or facts; a sequence of symbols to which meaning may be assigned

database—a structured electronic media storage repository for data, usually stored on a computer system, which uses a formal indexing structure that permits rapid retrieval of individual data elements from the database

database administrator—the person responsible for managing or administering a database system, particularly for defining the rules by which data are accessed, modified, and stored

database management program—*see DBMS*

database management system—*see DBMS*

database manager—*see database administrator*

data compression—the process of eliminating empty fields, gaps, redundancies, and unnecessary data to shorten the length of records or blocks so they take up less space when stored or transmitted

data corruption—a deliberate or accidental violation of data integrity

data dictionary—a centralized repository of information about the data stored in a database, providing definitions of data elements and data characteristics, relationship to other data, origin, usage and format; the data dictionary is a vital part of the database management system; *see DD*

data diddling—unauthorized alteration of data; a common form of computer crime

data encryption standard—an algorithm implemented in electronic hardware devices that is used to protect computer data through cryptography; used to protect data sent through an insecure system; *see DES*

data envelopment analysis—*see DEA*

data exchange—securing transmissions over communication channels

data flow diagram—*see DFD*

data independence—the ability to make changes to the logical or physical structure of data without changing the application programs that manipulate these data; to achieve data independence, system design should be performed in such a way as to keep the data basically separate from the application code

data integrity—protection of data from compromise and alteration, which may be either accidental or deliberate

data leakage—the nearly undetectable loss of control over or possession of information, such as by theft of data storage devices or unauthorized copying of files

data link layer—second layer in the OSI model; consists of upper logical link control (LLC) and lower media access control (MAC) portions; handles data flow control, the packaging of raw bits in frames or frames into raw data bits, and retransmits frames as needed; provides CRC error detection; bridges operate at this layer; *see LLC, and MAC*

data management component—major subsystem of a decision support system consisting of the database and the database management system

data mining—analysis of large stores of data to discover patterns in the data and to reveal associations between outputs (e.g., health status at discharge) and inputs (e.g., health status at admission, patient data); data mining algorithms cull through medical data to find these associations

data originator—the person who generates data, such as the patient for data related to symptoms, the physician for data related to the examination and decisions, and the nurse for patient care details

data origin authentication—corroboration that the data received has not been changed or altered in any way

data overflow—an internally represented date with a software product that reflects a base date and time, together with an offset in days, seconds, or microseconds since the base date and time

data processing—*see DP*

data/record linkage—bringing together two separately recorded pieces or sets of information concerning a particular individual, family, provider, or facility

data retrieval—to extract data from a storage medium for use or presentation, through the distribution of the data to the authorized user when and where they are needed

data security—to ensure that only authorized users can access the data by instituting an access control mechanism, such as passwords or other electronically unique evidence of user authorization

data service unit—*see DSU*

data set ready—*see DSR*

data subject—the person whose information is stored in the computer

data terminal ready—*see DTR*

data user—the person or organization that has justified need for certain data in order to perform legitimate tasks

date of service—*see DOS*

days per thousand—same as bed days/1000; a standard unit of measurement of utilization of health care services; refers to an annualized use of the hospital or other institutional care; the number of hospital days used in a year for each 1000 covered lives; derived by first taking the number of bed days divided by member months, and then multiplying by each 1000 members, also multiplied by the number of months under consideration

Daytona—Microsoft's code name for the Windows NT 3.5 operating system

DBMS—database management system; a software program or set of programs used to define, administer, retrieve, modify, delete, or insert data within a database and its applications, often with the objective to economically reduce data redundancy

DCE—distributed computing environment

DCG—diagnostic cost groups; a system of Medicare reimbursement for HMOs with risk contracts in which enrollees are classified into various DCGs on the basis of each beneficiary's prior 12-month hospitalization history

DD—data dictionary; a detailed compilation of data elements with information on the meaning, use, and authorization of users of the data elements

DDN—defense data network; packet switching network that integrated the ARPANET and MILNET and served the Department of Defense

DEA—data envelopment analysis; a single-objective linear programming-based technique used to benchmark and compare performance of single objectives of comparable units

debit card—a card used for drawing cash from machines and/or paying for retail purchases; unlike credit cards, debit cards are linked to current (i.e., checking or savings) accounts

debugging—the process of discovering and eliminating errors and defects (bugs) in program code

DEC—Digital Equipment Corporation; computer manufacturer synonymous with PDP, VAX, and Alpha machines

decision support system—*see DSS*

decision tree—a method of making decisions through structuring knowledge in a hierarchical tree-like fashion

Decmon.dll—Windows NT print monitor function for print jobs delivered to DEC-based printers

DECnet—Digital Equipment Corporation Network; phased network and protocol component used by DEC for LAN and WAN implementations associated with VAX and VMS; each phase is different from the other

decryption—the process of decoding an encrypted message so that its meaning becomes clear; the reverse process of encryption in which cipher text is transformed back into plain text using a second complex function and a decryption key

deductible—the minimum threshold payment that must be made by the enrollee each year before the plan begins to make payments on a shared or total basis; the amount the Loss of Plan must sustain for each member in each contract year for each category of coverage before any benefits become payable under the agreement; if an enrollee has a $100 annual deductible, no payment assistance comes from the plan until at least a total of $101 in eligible claims are processed within the calendar or contract year; plans will typically reduce the deductible if they wish to create an added incentive for patients to enroll, or they use reduced deductibles as the initial means to get reluctant patients to try some form of managed care

deductible carry-over credit—for plans that include a carry-over credit, the acceptable health care charges for services during the last three months of a calendar year may be used as a credit toward the next year's deductible

defamation—false written or oral communication to someone other than the subject of the defamation of matters that concern a living person and tend to injure that person's reputation

default gateway—TCP/IP configuration option that specifies a device or computer to send packets out of a local subnet; *see gateway*

Defense Data Network—*see DDN*

degaussing—exposure to high magnetic fields; one method of destroying data on a disk

delete—the removal of an enrollee from a health care plan, according to stated procedures or time limitations within the contract

deliberate threat—threat of a person or persons to damage a computer system consciously and willingly

delinquent claim—insurance claim submitted to an insurance company, for which payment is overdue; claim not submitted on time to a carrier

demodulation—reverse of modulation; the analog to digital signal conversion process occurring in a modem at a receiving site; analog signals are used to transfer data over phone lines; digital signals are used by the computer

denial-of-service attack—an attack in which a user (or a program) takes up so much of a shared resource that it is not available for other users or uses, or non-availability because of a disruption on the network due to a component failure or a software bug

dependent—an enrolled health plan member who has coverage tied to that of the sponsor; may be a spouse or an unmarried child, or a stepchild or legally adopted child of either the employee or the employee's spouse, whose primary domicile is with the employee, except for other arrangements as approved by the plan; often dependent children status is also delineated by those under the age of 18, or children attending college full-time under a specified age

DES—data encryption standard; technique for encrypting data; third-most secure option for RAS dial-in connections in Windows NT through the use of a 56-bit key

device—any piece of equipment used in computer input/output operations

DFD—data flow diagram; documentation of the logical design of an information system by graphically showing how data flow to, from, and within an information system, through the use of standard design symbols

DHCP—Dynamic Host Configuration Protocol; standard protocol that allows a network device to obtain all network IP configuration information automatically from host-based pooled IP addresses; alleviates manual static IP address assignment

diagnosis protocols—a subset of medical protocols that deal with the detection of disease; protocols outline a recommended set of examinations and tests, with corresponding index of diagnosis alternatives that are likely to be present, based upon the results; *see also medical protocols, prevention protocols, and treatment protocols*

DICOM—digital imaging and communications in medicine; *see DICOM standard*

DICOM Committee—Digital Imaging and Communications in Medicine; a standards board consisting of vendors, academics, and physicians.

DICOM Standard—a standard which involves the format and exchange of digital images and related information, to include network connections; a joint standard effort between users and industry now encompassing CT, MRI, nuclear medicine, ultrasound, and computed radiography

digital—*see digital signal*

Digital Equipment Corporation—*see DEC*

Digital Equipment Corporation Network—*see DECnet*

digital signal—transmission signal that carries information in the discrete value form of either 0 or 1, also referred to as either "on" or "off"

digital signal 0—*see DS-0*

digital signal 1—*see DS-1*

digital signal 2—*see DS-2*

digital signal 3—*see DS-3*

digital signature—guarantee of the authenticity of a set of input data the same way a written signature verifies the authenticity of a paper document; an encryption transformation of data that allows a recipient of the data to verify the source and integrity of the data and protect against forgery; any modification to the document after it is "signed" will cause the signature verification to fail (integrity); if the signature was computed using a private key other than the one corresponding to the public key used for verification, the verification will fail (authentication); *see private key and public key*

digital signature standard—*see DSS*

digitize—conversion of analog signal to a digital signal

digitized signature—an electronic image of a written signature; a digitized signature looks much the same as the original, but it does not provide the same protection as a digital signature, as it can be forged and copied

DII—Defense Information Infrastructure; consists of communications networks, computers, software, databases, applications, and other capabilities that meet the information processing, storage, and communications needs of Department of Defense users

DIP switch—dual in-line package switch; a grouping of small on (1)/off (0) switches used in computers and associated devices to configure hardware options

direct memory access—*see DMA*

direct memory access controller—*see DMA controller*

disaster plan—a plan that provides direction and guidelines to protect information from damage, minimize disruption, ensure stability, and provide for orderly recovery in the event of a disaster, etc.; the Joint Commission requires that accredited facilities develop a management plan that addresses emergency preparedness

disaster recovery—the process whereby any loss of data in the event of fire, vandalism, natural disaster, or system failure would be restored

discharge planning—the activity that occurs early in the admission process to evaluate the patient's medical needs in order to reduce LOS and to arrange for appropriate care after discharge from an inpatient setting, to include selection of LTC, sub-acute, home health, transportation, and other support service requirements; before specific emphasis was recently placed on discharge planning, patients often were ready for discharge from an acute hospital setting but still required care from a lower point along the continuum—but because plans had not been made in advance and no facility was available on short notice, patients were forced to remain in the hospital at a higher cost than would have been necessary within an alternative setting; *see also LOS and continuum of care*

discharge summary—an admission summary prepared at the time of the patient's discharge from the hospital

disclosure—making data available or allowing it to be obtained; the release of information to third parties within or outside the organization from an individual's record file with or without the consent of the individual to whom the record pertains

disenrollment—the process of terminating coverage; normally, voluntary disenrollment is not allowed until the patient has remained within the plan for at least 6-12 months; a patient can be involuntarily disenrolled because of a change in employment; Medicare seniors may disenroll at the beginning of any given month, assuming notice is given by a certain preceding deadline during the previous month

disk—rotating magnetic device used for file storage; can be magnetic floppy disk (diskette), hard disk, or optical CD

disk duplexing—a fault-tolerant storage technique that copies information simultaneously on a primary disk drive and a secondary hard drive on two separate channels; so, for a redundant strategy, if a failure occurs on one channel, the other is safeguarded; the file server response time is also faster because when "read" information is requested, the request is sent to whichever disk can respond faster; two disks and two disk controllers are required for disk duplexing; RAID 1

disk mirroring—a fault-tolerant storage technique that copies data on a primary disk drive and a secondary drive on the same channel, with more limited protection than in disk duplexing; two physical disks are required for mirroring; RAID 1

disk operating system—*see DOS*

disk striping without parity—*see RAID 0*

disk striping with parity—*See RAID 5*

diskette—small, flexible, removable, magnetic storage media used for file storage; available in 3.5-inch (720 KB, 1.44 MB and 2.88 MB of storage) and 5.25-inch (360 KB and 1.2 MB of storage) sizes; previously available in an 8-inch size

disposable smart cards—cards with a predetermined cash value that cannot be reloaded with funds after the specified amount of funds has been used, i.e., $10 telephone cards

distributed computing—*see distributed processing*

distributed computing environment (DCE)—a client-server environment that is independent of the operating system and network and in which data are located in more than one server that might be geographically dispersed, but connected by a wide-area network (WAN)

distributed database—a database that is stored in more than one physical location or on more than one server; parts of the database are physically stored in one location, while other parts are stored and maintained in other locations

distributed processing—the distribution of computer processing work among multiple servers linked by a communications network, e.g. LAN or WAN

DLC—dynamic link control; protocol used with networked enabled HP printers and for connectivity to IBM mainframe machines from Windows NT

DMA—direct memory access; rapid data movement of data between computer subsystems; accomplished through the use of the DMA controller without the use of the CPU

DMA Controller—direct memory access controller; integrated computer chip that handles direct memory operations without

CPU intervention; allows the CPU to concentrate on other computer operations

DNS—domain name service; an on-line database that maps network addresses to more easily read Internet addresses

DNSSEC—secure domain name service for authentication and integrity

domain—collection of Windows NT servers and workstations under the same name and control; there are four domain types: Single, Master, Multiple Master, and Complete Trust

domain controller—Windows NT server that authenticates users and maintains a security accounts database; can be a primary domain controller (PDC) or backup domain controller (BDC)

domain name system—*see DNS*

domain synchronization—Windows NT process where a primary domain controller (PDC) updates all backup domain controllers (BDCs) with an updated copy of the accounts database through the replication service; default PDC to BDC synchronization occurs every five minutes; BDCs can also be manually synchronized with the PDC through server manager

DOS—date of service; the day of health care service to an enrolled beneficiary

DOS—disk operating system; set of 16-bit software programs that direct system-level computer operation

DP—data processing; technologies to support the automation of routines that support administrative and decision operations

DRAM—dynamic RAM; RAM that must be continuously refreshed to maintain the current RAM value; most RAM in microcomputers is dynamic RAM B, although there is a trend toward SDRAM

DRG—diagnosis- or diagnostic-related group; a Yale University-derived system of classification for 383 inpatient hospital services based on principal diagnosis, secondary diagnosis, surgical procedures, age, sex, and presence of complications; this system is used as a financing mechanism to reimburse hospitals and selected other providers for services rendered; used to describe patient mix in hospitals and to determine hospital reimbursement policy

drill down analysis—method of detailing certain key information in a hierarchical format to give users the ability to work down to greater levels of detail within an automated system

drop—wiring run made from a modular wall plate to a comm/ wiring closet; UTP is the most common medium used in drops; also identified as the connection between a computer and thicknet cabling

DS-0—digital signal 0; 64 Kbps synchronous digital transmission

DS-1—digital signal 1; 1.544 Mbps synchronous digital transmission

DS-2—digital signal 2; 6.312 Mbps synchronous digital transmission

DS-3—digital signal 3; 45 Mbps synchronous digital transmission

DSR—data set ready; modem control that indicates that the modem is attached to a communications line

DSS—digital signature standard; an emerging technology for ensuring data integrity and authentication of the sender and content that employs cryptography to make electronic signature unforgeable; the signatures are electronically linked to the individual document with a time and date stamp to prevent tampering and alteration

DSS—decision support system; a relatively new discipline and family of software applications that link together necessary data and applications containing models, in order to enhance leadership's ability to solve problems or make decisions

DSU—data service unit; provides digital-to-digital communication; *see CSU/DSU*

DTR—data terminal ready; modem control that indicates a terminal is ready for transmission

dual eligible—used to describe a beneficiary eligible for Medicare and Medicaid, and under the proposed MediGrant policy would be eligible for Medicare and MediGrant within a set aside program funding; used within the Department of Defense to describe a beneficiary that has dual health care entitlement as both a military retiree and a Medicare eligible

dual in-line package switch—*see DIP switch*

dual-use technology—technology that has both civilian and military applications, i.e., cryptography

dumb terminal—terminal with no localized processing, storage, or GUI capability; VT-320s, VT-420s, and VT-510s are dumb terminals associated with CHCS; mainly associated with mainframes and centralized computing

dumpster diving—searching through trash looking for discarded information that can provide clues to probable passwords; used by people desiring to gain access to a computer system

duplication of benefits or coverage—partially or totally duplicate coverage under two or more plans for the same potential loss, usually the result of contracts with different service organizations, insurance companies, or prepayment plans

DXNNH—diagnosis not normally hospitalized

Dynamic Host Configuration Protocol—*see DHCP*

dynamic link control—*see DLC*

dynamic RAM—*see DRAM*

E-1—European digital signal 1; 2.048 Mbps digital transmission that is similar to ISDN

E-2—European digital signal 2; 34.368 Mbps digital transmission that is similar to ISDN

E-3—European digital signal 3; 139.254 Mbps digital transmission that is similar to ISDN

EBCDIC—Extended Binary Coded Decimal Interchange Code; eight-bit standard information processing code developed by IBM that is used extensively with mainframe magnetic tape units

E codes—a classification of ICD-9-CM coding for external causes of injury rather than disease; E codes are also used in coding adverse reactions to medications

EDI—electronic data interchange; transmission of business data via computer can be used in the health arena to exchange eligibility information, claims, encounters, and other data needed to manage contracts and remittance

EDLIN—line editor; used with early releases of DOS to edit text files

EEPROM—electronically erasable programmable read only memory; a reprogrammable memory chip that can be electronically erased and reprogrammed via a reader/writer device

EGA—enhanced graphics adapter; color display system providing 16 to 64 colors at a resolution of 640 x 480; not supported by Windows 95 and Windows NT

EGP—Exterior Gateway Protocol; advertises the networks that can be reached within an autonomous system by advertising its IP addresses to a router in another autonomous system; no longer used

EIDE—enhanced or extended integrated drive electronics; a standard interface for high-speed disk drives that operates at speeds faster than the standard IDE interface; it allows the connection of four IDE devices

EIN—employer identification number; recommended by the Department of Health and Human Services as the standard identification for employers, similar to the employee social security number; the EIN will be public information

EIS—executive information system; a system in which executives are able to conduct on-line queries and analyze trends for specific performance items, track exception reports, drill down specific indicators, and access and integrate a broad range of internal and external organizational data to understand what is going on in an area of the organization; *see also ESS*

EISA—extended industry standard architecture; 32-bit internal bus; introduced in 1988 to compete with the PS/2 (Micro Channel) line of computers

electromagnetic interference (EMI)—any disruption caused by electromagnetic waves; *see also radio-frequency interference*

electronic claim—insurance claim submitted to the carrier by a central processing unit, tape diskette, direct data entry, direct wire, dial-in telephone, digital fax, or personal computer download or upload; *see also EDI*

electronic data interchange—*see EDI*

electronic mail—see E-mail.

electronic medical record—*see CPR*

electronic patient record—*see CPR*

electronic signature—the attribute that is applied to an electronic document to bind it to a particular entity or a person; ensures the integrity of the signed document; a signature on a document verifies the integrity of the document and the identity of the signer; technologies available for user authentication include passwords, cryptography, and biometrics

eligibility date—the day on which an enrollee is first entitled to health care benefits according to a contract

eligibility list—a list that shows the eligible enrolled members for health care services and supplies, including their effective date

eligibility period—time following the eligibility date (usually 31 days) during which a member of an insured group may apply for insurance without evidence of insurability

eligible employee—health plan contracts outline an employee's eligibility requirements, which are based on such factors as full-time or part- time employment as stipulated in the contract

eligible dependent—*see dependent*

eligible expenses—the usual, customary, and reasonable charges or established rates for health care or supplies covered or allowed under a health plan; do not include copayments to any source, or amounts paid by the member under the membership service agreement

eligible hospital services—medically necessary hospital services that are provided to a member in a hospital on a day for which there is a room and board charge, prescribed by a licensed physician, and rendered according to the membership service agreement; include referral services, but they are not deemed to include physicians' or surgeons' charges unless specifically included in an endorsement

ELOC—executable lines of code; source lines of codes minus the comments, white-space, and data declarations; the unit of measure used in costing models to capture the effort to create the functional portion of a software program and often used to cost the effort of developing functionality, such as function point analysis

e-mail—electronic mail; electronic messages sent via networks between users on other computer systems

emergency repair disk—*see ERD*

EMI—electromagnetic interference

employer identification number—*see EIN*

EMR—electronic medical record; *see CPR*

emulation—software program that allows a computer to imitate another computer with a different operating system

encryption—a process by which a message is encoded so that its meaning is not clear; it is transformed into a coded message using a complex function and a special encryption key

enhanced graphics adapter—*see EGA*

enhanced integrated drive electronics—*see EIDE*

enhanced small device interface—*see ESDI*

enrollee—a covered member of a health care contract, who is eligible to receive contract services; *see also insured*

enrollee health status measures—indicators of a health plan's ability to maintain the health of its enrollee population

enrollment—the number of patients who have contracted with a carrier; the process or activity of actually recruiting and signing up individuals and groups for membership in a plan; a description of the number of covered lives in a plan

enrollment card—a card-type document that serves as notice that an employee wishes to participate in an employer group insurance plan

enterprise network—network consisting of multiple servers and domains over a small or large geographical area

enterprise network services—examples are security, messaging, administration, host connectivity, and wide-area network communication

episode—includes all health care treatment and expenditures surrounding an admission as an inpatient, partial hospitalization, or outpatient treatment; the analysis of episode costs are generally conducted by selecting some reasonable but arbitrary period of time surrounding the event, and relating all costs to that episode, such as treatment between admission and discharge, or any care received within 14 days from the day of admission

EPR—*see CPR*

EPROM—erasable programmable memory; reusable firmware that can be reprogrammed; previous contents are erased by applying ultraviolet light through the window in the chip

erasable programmable memory—*see EPROM*

ERD—emergency repair disk; Windows NT floppy disk that contains machine-specific repair process information on registry (system, software, security, SAM) and system files (ntuser.da_, autoexec.nt, config.nt, setup.log, default._) for use when failures occur; nonbootable diskette, must be used with Windows NT setup disks

ERISA—Employee Retirement Income Security Act; this 1974 federal law mandates reporting and disclosure requirements for group life and health plans, with relevant guidance on the sponsorship, administration, minimum record retention period, servicing of plans, some claims processing, appeals regulations, and minimum mandatory clinical benefits; ERISA removes self-insured health plans from the various state legislation regarding health insurance

ERISA plan—within the context of insurance benefits for employees [29 U.S.C., 1002(1)], ERISA plans provide for the variety of medical, surgical, hospitalization, disability, death, unemployment, and other benefits

ESDI—Enhanced Small Device Interface; short-lived hard disk drive interface standard introduced by Compaq; step in technology after MFM but before IDE

ESS—executive support system; extends all of the capabilities of an EIS and has additional capabilities to augment the strategic decision-making and forecasting roles of senior management;

intended as a flexible tool to provide information support and analysis capability for a wide range of executive strategic decisions.

Ethernet—a 10 Mbps LAN specification developed jointly by Xerox, Intel, and Digital Equipment corporations

Ethernet 802.3—*see IEEE 802.3; see also CSMA/CD*

European digital signal 1—*see E-1*

European digital signal 2—*see E-2*

European digital signal 3—*see E-3*

even parity—method of data parity that uses an even number of "1" bits in each byte or word; the parity bit is set for an even number of 1 bits

Event Viewer—Windows NT utility that captures and displays system, application, and security error conditions; all users can access the system and application logs, and only those with administrator access can view the security logs

Exabyte—1024 terabytes

exception—a transaction that does not receive authorization by the accepted rules and procedures

executable lines of code—*see ELOC*

executive information system—*see EIS*

executive support system—*see ESS*

expanded memory—additional area of memory beyond the conventional 640 KB associated with DOS machines

expert system—a software application that contains expert knowledge about a particular problem, often in the form of a set of "if-then" rules, that is able to solve problems at a level equivalent or greater than human experts; early medical applications serve the area of automated medical diagnoses; *see also case-based reasoning and AI*

expressed consent—oral or written agreement; because it is difficult to prove that oral consent was given, most expressed consent is expected to be recorded with a signature

Extended American Standard Code for Information Interchange—*see Extended ASCII*

Extended ASCII—Extended American Standard Code for Information Interchange; extensively used eight-bit standard information processing code with 256 characters

Extended Binary Coded Decimal Interchange Code—*see EBCDIC*

extended industry standard architecture—*see EISA*

extended integrated drive electronics—*see EIDE*

extended memory—additional area of memory beyond 1 MB associated with DOS machines (EMS)

extended semantics for Y2K—specific values for a date field are reserved for special interpretation, with "99" commonly in a two-digit year field as an indefinite end date that does not expire

Extended Technology—*see XT*

Exterior Gateway Protocol—*see EGP*

face sheet—*see discharge summary*

facsimile technology—*see fax*

Fair Information Practices—a set of principles originally set forth in 1973 that governs the collection and use of information about individuals and forms the basis of most United States and European privacy law

family set—group of backup tapes consisting of a single run of backup information

fast SCSI—fast small computer system interface; 10 Mbps high-speed eight-bit bus interface for connecting devices to the computer bus; pronounced "scuzzy"

fast small computer system interface—*see fast SCSI*

FAT—file allocation table; 16-bit file cluster system technique used by MS-DOS and Windows operating systems to manage disk space; can also be used with Windows NT

FAT32—file allocation table 32-bit; 32-bit file system technique used by the Windows 95 operating systems to manage disk space; cannot be used with Windows NT

fax—the reproduction of an image or document, short for facsimile; to send or receive documents between locations on a telecommunications network

fax server—a network service or devices that gives a local area network (LAN) workstation the access to incoming or outgoing faxes across the LAN

FDDI—fiber distributed data interface; fiber optic dual token ring network, and variable sized packet sizes through shared local area network connection; provides the transfer data rate up to 100 million bits per second, or 100 MHz of bandwidth at a distance of 200 km

Federal Privacy Act of 1974—U.S.C. Sec. 552a (1988)

fee for service—*see FFS*

fee schedule—under a fee-for-service arrangement, or discounted FFS, the fee schedule is the document which outlines all predetermined fee maximums that the participating provider will be paid by the health plan within the period of the contract; *see also Medicare fee schedule*

FFS—fee-for-service; the full rate of charge for a patient without any type of insurance arrangement, discounted arrangement, or prepaid health plan; before managed care this was the typical mechanism for pay for care; serious problems of cost containment under this traditional reimbursement setting included churning and coding creep, in addition to charges that may have been excessive in relation to the actual cost of providing care or services

fiber distributed data interface—*see FDDI*

fiber optic cable—a pure glass cable used for the transmission of digital signals; it generates no radiation of its own and is resistant to electromagnetic interference; it is used in areas where security is of prime importance because taps to the cable are detectable; it can be used over longer distances than copper cable

fiber optics—extremely fast communications technology that uses a glass or plastic medium to transmit light pulses produced by LEDs or ILDs to represent data; immune to EMI but susceptible to chromatic dispersion

fiber transceiver—device that converts fiber optic signals to digital signals and vice versa; usually used to make a connection from a fiber run to an Ethernet segment

field level security—data protection of specified fields within files rather than of entire files; authorization to access only specified fields rather than entire files

FIFO—first in first out; a queue scheduling method that executes the first in process or order received requests, or in the order received

file—electronic data collected in related records

file allocation table—*see FAT*

file allocation table 32-bit—*see FAT32*

File and Print Services for NetWare—*see FPNW*

file server—networked computer that provides file handling and storage for users with network access; a computer that each computer on a network can use to access and retrieve files that are shared among the attached computers; access to files is controlled by the file server's software rather than by the operating system of the computer that accesses the file

File Transfer Protocol—*see FTP*

FIP—*see Fair Information Practices*

firewall—hardware and software components that protect one set of system resources from attack by outside network users by blocking and checking all incoming network traffic; firewalls permit authorized users to access and transmit privileged information and deny access to unauthorized users

firmware—computer instructions written to a read-only ROM, PROM, or EPROM chip

first in first out—*see FIFO*

first-level T-carrier digital trunk—*see T-1*

flash memory—nonvolatile memory that provides read-only operations for computer boot-up; contents can be updated

flash memory—smart card memory technology that emulates a hard disk, except that the data are stored electronically, and there are no moving parts; it erases and writes data by blocks (groups of bytes)

flat files—computer files in which each record has the same length whether or not all the space is used; empty parts of the record contain blanks or zeroes, depending on the data type of each field; files are not compressed to save storage space

flaw—a weak point in a computer program that does not impact the performance of the program but which may allow a hacker unauthorized access to a computer system

flip-flop—digital logical circuit that can store one bit of information or be in a cleared state; one bit memory

foreground—application or task that is executing and accepting user input and subsequent output on a multitasking machine

Fortezza Card—a credit-card-size electronic module that stores digital information that can be recognized by a network or system; it is used to provide data encryption and authentication services

fourth-generation language—*see 4GL*

fourth-level T-Carrier digital trunk—*see T-4*

FPNW—File and Print Services for NetWare; provides the ability to make Windows NT server resources available to NetWare clients

fractional T-1—fractional first-level T-Carrier digital trunk; provides a subdivision of a T-1 circuit; a portion of the T-1's 1.544 Mbps bandwidth is available

frame—a packet that can be 64 to 1518 bytes long and contains header/data/trailer information in addition to a preamble to mark the start of a frame

frame relay—a packet-oriented communication method used for local area network (LAN) interconnection and wide area network (WAN) connections; used in both private and public networks

Freedom of Information Act—requires that records pertaining to the executive branch of the federal government be available to the public except for matters that fall within exempted areas, including "medical files and similar files, the disclosure of which would constitute a clearly unwarranted invasion of personal privacy"

FTP—File Transfer Protocol; protocol allowing the network movement of files from node to node or system to system over a TCP/IP network; used to send files from one system to another as commanded by a user, e.g. downloading files from a remote server

full duplex—communication channel/circuit that allows simultaneous two-way data transmission

functional requirements—a statement of the system behavior needed to enforce a given policy; requirements are used to derive the technical specifications of a system; describes what you want the system to perform

fuzzy logic—an artificial intelligence method for making decisions with imprecisely specified knowledge; for example, defining loose boundaries to distinguish 'low' from 'high' values; *see also AI*

fuzzy-set theory—a theory that entails specifying a patient's possible disease state by tracking an upper and lower bound value, using applied fuzzy logic, for constraining the patient's symptomatology and disease parameters

garbage in garbage out—*see GIGO*

gateway—device or application that interconnects two services or two dissimilar networks providing protocol translation between them; a protocol converter; a device that directs computer information traffic and connects two computer networks that use different communications architectures; often used to connect a network under the control of one organization (an internal network) with a network controlled by another organization (an external network); gateways are natural points at which to enforce access control policies

Gateway Services for NetWare—*see GSNW*

GB—gigabyte

Gbps—gigabits per second; transmission of a billion bits per second

GHz—gigahertz; one billion cycles per second

GIF—graphics interchange format; standard for encoding, transmitting, decoding, and providing photo quality images; introduced by CompuServe in 1987

Gigabit—one billion bits

Gigabyte—approximately one billion bytes (1024 megabytes); unit of computer storage capacity

Gigahertz—*see GHz*

GIGO—garbage in garbage out; synonymous with the entry of inaccurate or useless data and the processed output of worthless/useless information

global internet communication—includes e-mail, voice mail, group and desktop videoconferencing, Internetphones, videophones, and high-speed cable systems to support holographic telepresence

global system of mobility—*see GSM*

gopher—text-based, menu-driven, document-retrieval information service used on the Internet; has virtually been made obsolete by the introduction of graphical-based web browsers; a tool for locating data on the Internet that enables the user to locate textual information stored on Internet servers through a series of search and retrieve menus

granularity—an expression of the relative size of a unit; the smallest discrete information that can be directly retrieved; in security, it is the degree of protection that can be achieved; protection at the file level is considered coarse granularity; granularity at a single user is fine granularity because access-control can be adjusted to include or exclude any single user

Graphics Interchange Format—see GIF

Groupware—Network software that defines applications used by a group of people. Allows users on different systems to collaborate and interact. Electronic mail is an example.

GSM—global system of mobility; a digital cell phone international standard for architecture and operation, which applies to packet-data messaging, voice, and data

GSNW—Gateway Services for NetWare; provides the ability to connect to and make NetWare server resources available to a Windows NT server

GUI—graphical user interface; the part of a computer system that users interact with that uses graphic icons and a mouse to issue commands to the computer and make selections of what files are going to be used; uses an interface that employs graphical images for the execution of resources as opposed to command line entry; employs windows, icons, and menus in lieu of text to run programs

H

hacker—a person who gains unauthorized access to a computer network

half duplex—communication channel/circuit that allows data transmission in both directions, in one direction at a time, but not in both directions simultaneously

hard copy—file printed to a paper document

hard disk—sealed magnetic storage unit employing high rpm platters for magnetic storage of files

hardware—the physical components of a computer system, versus the software programs, communications network, or data that are used by the computer.

hardware address—unique low-level address burned into each piece of network hardware

hardware compatibility list—*see HCL*

hashing—iterative process that computes a value (referred to as a hashword) from a particular data unit in a manner that, when the hashword is protected, makes manipulation of the data detectable

HCFA (Health Care Financing Administration) Common Procedure Coding System—*see HCPCS*

HCFA 1500—a standardized claim form, developed by HCFA, for providers of services to bill professional fees to health carriers or third parties; not used for hospital or institutional charges

HCL—hardware compatibility list; provides a list of devices supported by Windows NT

HCPCS—HCFA (Health Care Financing Administration) Common Procedure Coding System; a three-level alphanumeric set of codes used by HCFA to describe a series of provider services, supplies, and procedures; including CPT codes and also others that supplement CPT, such as Durable Medical Equipment (DME), ambulance services, and physical therapy; levels 1 and 2 [coding of the medical data to include Employer's Standard Identifier (ESI)/National Provider Identifier (NPI) and the type of care facility] will be adopted in the year 2000; further modifications will come in level 3; "J" drug codes have been eliminated from the original plan; *see also EIN and NPI*

HDSS—Health Decision Support System; any interactive human–computer system that is organized to provide easy access to a wide range of decision models, from basic analytical frameworks (e.g., automated spreadsheet models) to expert information systems (e.g., neural networks); a label given to a large class of intelligent information processing tools capable of providing enhanced management and clinical decision support not typically found in traditional health information systems and applications, which facilitates the decision maker's use of data and models to solve problems or answer questions

health care information—information contained in a patient record; information about the patient generated and maintained in providing health care services

health care information system—*see HIS*

health decision support system—*see HDSS*

health level 7—*see HL7*

health management information system—*see HMIS*

health professionals—physicians (doctors of medicine and doctors of osteopathy), dentists, nurses, podiatrists, optometrists, physicians' assistants, clinical psychologists, social workers, pharmacists, nutritionists, occupational therapists, physical therapists, and other professionals engaged in the delivery of health services who are licensed, practice under an institutional license, are certified, or practice under authority of the HMO, a medical group, IPA, or other authority consistent with state law

health promotion—activities by an individual educator, physician, provider group, IDS, or HMO, that are oriented toward providing the patient or enrolled population with various educational materials, lectures, health risk assessments and appraisals, incentives or disincentives, or interactive discussion settings that create awareness of healthy lifestyles; teaching the population how to remain healthy and keep costs low; may include self-care and proper use of a PCP or care options; most programs include smoking, weight control, exercise, eating habits, stress, cholesterol, and blood pressure

health selection—an artifactual explanation of a socioeconomic gradient in health suggesting that differences in health status are caused by socioeconomic factors

HEDIS—Health Plan Employer Data Information Set; the result of a coordinated development effort by NCQA to provide a group of 60 performance measures that gives employers some objective information with which to evaluate health plans and hold them accountable; HEDIS helps ensure that HMOs and purchasers of care are speaking the same language when they are comparing value and accountability

help desk—the nerve center of the daily information systems operation; depending upon the size of the supported organization, the help desk is responsible for receiving "trouble calls" from users, a hotline where problems are recorded and resolved, education and training, consultations, configuration support, and equipment ordering, in addition to the more traditional aspect of problem resolution; the help desk can work hand-in-hand with dispatched personnel from network engineering, PC, or workstation desk-side support

Hercules Graphics Card—*see HGC*

hertz—one cycle per second; CPUs are measured in MHz; abbreviated Hz; the number of electrical cycles that takes place on a channel within a second, or the frequency of a carrier signal on a channel; the frequency of a voice grade telephone line is 3 KHz, or the difference between the low frequency of 300 Hz and the high frequency of 3300 Hz; *see also bps*

hexadecimal—base 16 numbering system where four bits are used to represent each digit; uses the 0–9 digits and A–F letters for the representations of the 10–15 digits

HGC—Hercules Graphics Card; monochrome graphics display at a resolution of 720 x 348; display type used before CGA and EGA

HHS—United States Department of Health and Human Services

hidden layer(s)—group of neurons organized in layer(s) between input and output neurons; usually one hidden layer is used, although a neural network can have more than one hidden layer

hidden node—the neuron located in a hidden layer

high level language—*see HLL*

high performance file system—*see HPFS*

hijacking—the ability of a hacker to misuse a system by gaining entry through a computer of a user who failed to log off from a previous use

HIPAA—Health Insurance Portability and Accountability Act of 1996; requires the Department of Health and Human Services to establish security standards and safeguards for the electronic transmission of certain health information; 11 standards are now proposed for health claims, health encounter information, health claims attachments, health plan enrollment and disenrollment, health plan eligibility, health care payment and remittance advice, coordination of benefits and sequential processing of claims, health plan premium payments, first report of injury, health claim status, and referral certification and authorization

HIS—health care or hospital information system; generally used to describe hospital computer systems with functions like general ledger, master patient index, electronic patient record, patient admission and discharge, order entry for laboratory tests or medications, billing, and other software applications

hive—a section of registry information

HKEY_CLASSES_ROOT—one of five Windows NT registry keys; maintains OLE (object linking & embedding) information and file associations; maintains compatibility with Windows 3.1

HKEY_CURRENT_CONFIG— one of five Windows NT registry keys; maintains information about the current configuration of the computer

HKEY_CURRENT_MACHINE— one of five Windows NT registry keys; maintains information about the software and hardware configuration that does not change between operating system loads

HKEY_CURRENT_USER—one of five Windows NT registry keys; maintains information about the current logged on user(s) preferences

HKEY_USERS—one of five Windows NT registry keys; maintains information about all users who have logged on to a particular machine; where cached credentials are maintained

HL7—health level seven; a communication protocol that is unique to the medical information field, used for data exchange between computer applications; the term "level seven" refers to the highest level of the Open System Interconnection (OSI) model of the International Standards Organization (ISO); in the OSI conceptual model, the communications functions are separated into seven levels; this standard is primarily focused on the issues that occur within the seventh, or application, level; the standard currently addresses the interfaces among various systems that send or receive patient admissions/registration, discharge or transfer admission discharge or transfer (ADT) data, queries, orders, results, clinical observations, billing, and master file update information; the next version of the standard (2.3) will expand on the current coverage of these areas and will include new coverage for patient care, medical records, and automated instruments; work is also underway to produce HL7 standards for recording immunizations and drug reactions

HLL—high level language; a language with instructions that combine several machine level instructions into one instruction; *see also VHLL*

HMIS—health management information system; the application of a total systems perspective in linking relevant theoretical principles with practical methodologies and their applications to improve health service delivery within the context of current and future health care environments

holographic—characteristic of a whole being embedded in the whole's parts so that any part can be used to reconstitute the whole

home page—a document on the Internet or World Wide Web that acts as a front page or point of welcome to a series of embedded HTML documents, audio/video links, or other information; *see also Internet*

hop—unit of distance when comparing device routes; measure of distance between one router to another

hop count—number of hops from one node to another; number of routers that must be transversed to reach a destination

hospital information system—*see HIS*

host—a computer that is connected to at least one network; computer in a centralized computer model that is used via time-share by terminals connected to it for processing

HOSTS file—text file that maps remote host names to IP addresses; acts as a local DNS equivalent to provide a static type of DNS service

HPFS—High Performance File System; OS/2 operating system file system; Windows NT 3.x supports HPFS, but Windows NT 4.0 no longer supports this file system; it must be converted with the CONVERT command for use with Windows NT 4.0

Hpmon.dll—Windows NT print monitor for print jobs delivered to HP printers

HTML—Hypertext Markup Language; the description language used to create hypertext documents so they can be displayed on the Internet; ASCII-based language used for creating files and to display documents or web pages to web browsers

HTTP—Hypertext Transfer Protocol; communication link protocol used by WWW servers and browsers to transfer/exchange

HTML documents over the Internet; the format used for interacting with web pages (i.e., requests and receipts of messages)

hub—electronic network device to which multiple networked computers are attached; divides a data channel into two or more channels of lower bandwidth; hubs function at the physical layer (first layer) of the OSI model; also called a concentrator or receptor; *see concentrator*

hybrid network—type of LAN topology where networked nodes are connected to hubs where star and ring topologies are combined into one overall topology

hybrid smart card—a card that combines both optical and smart card technologies

hyperlink—a connection between hypertext documents that allows a browser to link concepts appearing in one document to related terms in other documents

hypertext—a method of preparing documents through a rapidly growing number of software applications that allows the text to be read and browsed in a manner that allows a "nonlinear" access to the material

Hypertext Transfer Protocol—*see HTTP*

Hypertext Markup Language—*see HTML*

Hz—*see Hertz*

IAP—Internet access provider; a company that provides basic Internet connection access; no additional services are provided

IBNR—incurred but not reported; represents revenue for a hospital or system that has a float type of accounting; contracts deal with IBNR, and may commit terms for this financial value of care by placing a certain amount of money in the providers account as recognition that care has already been rendered (although there is increasing pressure by HMOs to delete these reserves); may also refer to PCP referrals to specialists; care has been provided but the carrier has not received the claim yet; the carrier sets aside IBNR reserves to allow for the projected level of future liabilities during the lag period

ICC—integrated circuit chip

ICD-9—International Classification of Diseases 9th Revision; a statistical classification system consisting of a listing of diagnoses and identifying codes for reporting diagnosis of health plan enrollees identified by physicians; coding and terminology to accurately describe primary and secondary diagnosis and provide for consistent documentation for claims; the codes are revised periodically by the World Health Organization; since the Medicare Catastrophic Coverage Act of 1988, ICD-9 is mandatory for Medicare claims

icon—a small graphical object used in a GUI environment to execute a program; used in Windows, Windows 95, Windows NT, and OS/2 operating systems

iconic interface—a type of user interface using icons to represent actions and objects; the icons are manipulated by the user to achieve the desired navigation or result; *see also icon*

ICWS—Internet-base collaborative workgroup system; a customized system used by workgroup participants to achieve collaboration in work activities

IDE—integrated drive electronics; a standard ISA 16-bit bus interface for high-speed disk drives that operates at 5 Mbps with two attached devices (master and slave); invented in 1986 and introduced in microcomputers in 1989/1990

identification and authentication—use of a password or some other form of identification to screen users and check their authorization to use the system

identification card—a card that is commonly issued by an HMO or other health plan entity to identify each enrollee as being eligible, according to the contract coverage agreement

IEEE—Institute of Electrical and Electronic Engineers; a computer, electronics, and networking standards and specifications organization

IEEE 802—IEEE committee standard for defining networks at the physical and data link control layers of the OSI model

IEEE 802.1—IEEE committee standard for LAN architecture and internetworking

IEEE 802.2—IEEE committee standard for the logical link control (LLC) layer portion of the data link control layer

IEEE 802.3—IEEE committee standard for CSMA/CD Ethernet LANs; *see also CSMA/CD*

IEEE 802.4—IEEE committee standard for token-bus LANs

IEEE 802.5—IEEE committee standard for token-ring LANs

IEEE 802.6—IEEE committee standard for MANs

IEEE 802.8—IEEE committee standard for fiber optics

IEEE 802.11—IEEE committee standard for wireless LANs

IGP—Interior Gateway Protocol; *see RIP*

IIS—Internet information server; server that provides HTTP and FTP services to web browsers

ILD—injection laser diode; laser diode that provides the light pulses used with single mode fiber to convey data transmission information

imaging—the process of scanning and capturing, storing, displaying, and printing graphical information, such as the capturing of paper documents, on optical disks for archival purposes; can be used to store and call up documents from centralized image storage systems

IMD—information management department; department within a facility that provides data automation, hardware, software, and user support

implied consent—an action other than written consent on the part of a patient that demonstrates consent

industry standard architecture—*see ISA*

infiltration—entry into a computer system via the communication lines of an inactive user that is still connected to the computer; canceling a user's sign-off signal and then operating under his password and authorization; *see also piggyback*

information—data to which meaning is assigned, organized, interpreted, or structured according to context and assumed conventions in order to confer meaning

information compromise—an intentional or accidental disclosure or surrender of data to an unauthorized receiver

information infrastructure—the combination of computers and an information system

information management department—*see IMD*

information privacy—the right of a person to know that his/her recorded personal information is accurate, pertinent, complete, and up-to-date and that effective steps are in effect to restrict access to agreed upon purposes by authorized data users

information resource management—*see IRM*

information security—the result of effective protection measures that safeguard data or information, to prevent accidental or intentional disclosure to unauthorized persons, accidental or malicious alteration, unauthorized copying, loss by theft and/or destruction by computer system failures, or physical damage by fire, water, smoke, excessive temperature, electrical failure, or sabotage; the protection of the integrity, availability, and confidentiality of information and resources used to enter, store, process, and communicate the information

information superhighway—a fashionable term used to describe the Internet as a highway-type conveyer of electronic information

information systems—health care information systems requirements have undergone significant growth, requiring robust architecture to handle general ledger, claims processing and payment, membership enrollment, materials management, purchasing, ancillary services, home care, benefit management by plan/product/level, utilization review/utilization management, physician profiling, credentials, billing and accounts receivable, administrative support, etc.; systems are used to track, measure, analyze, and improve performance of providing clinical care and properly managing the financial performance of providing care

information warfare—deliberate attacks on the confidentiality and possession of data, its integrity, authenticity, availability, and usefulness

informed consent to disclosure—a freely given consent that follows a careful explanation by a caregiver to a patient or patient's representative of what information will be disclosed; understands the information being disclosed; is competent to provide consent; and consents willingly, not under coercion

injection laser diode—*see ILD*

inpatient days per thousand—*see days per thousand*

input layer—in neural network methodology, the input layer is a group of neurons that get input from example cases, not from other neurons

Institute of Electrical and Electronic Engineers—*see IEEE*

integrated call management—an important strategy to improve speed and efficiency in many health care applications through the use of multiple automated system components for telesystems support or medical information systems design; characterized by an open information systems architecture, which allows an organization to develop or add to systems that have been selected for their compatibility with a wide variety of other instruments or technology; automated call sequencers, call screen transfer capability, and voice response systems are only components within an integrated call management system

integrated drive electronics—*see IDE*

integrated services digital network (ISDN)—*see ISDN*

integrated services digital network basic rate—*see ISDN basic rate*

integrated services digital network primary rate—*see ISDN primary rate*

integration testing—testing to determine that the related information system components perform to the desired specification

interface—a boundary across which two systems communicate, which could be a hardware connector used to link devices, or a convention or protocol used to allow communication between two software systems; interfaces may be internal to the system, its applications, and programs, or other internal or external systems

integrity—knowledge that a message has not been modified while in transit; data integrity pertains to the accuracy and completeness of the data, program integrity, system integrity, and network integrity, which are all components of a computer or system security program

Interior Gateway Protocol—*see IGP*

International Classification of Diseases 9th Revision—*see ICD-9*

Internet—a global network interconnecting thousands of dissimilar computer networks and millions of computers worldwide, offering various services to users with browsing software (web browsers); the system that supports the use of multimedia hypertext coded documents that are available to users of the Internet

Internet access provider—*see IAP*

Internet-base collaborative workgroup system—*see ICWS*

Internet information server—*see IIS*

Internet layer—*see network layer*

Internet Network Information Center—*see InterNIC*

Internet protocol—specifications for the way data are divided up and reassembled during transmission; *see also IP*

Internet Protocol address—*see IP address*

Internet Protocol datagram—*see IP datagram*

Internet Protocol–next generation—*see IPng*

Internet service provider—*see ISP*

internetwork— a network of computer networks

internetwork packet exchange/sequence—*see IPX and SPX*

InterNIC—Internet Network Information Center; agency that provides and coordinates Internet services, such as IP addresses; also called the NIC

interoperability—the ability of a software application to exchange data and use information while operating on two different machine platforms and maintaining the identical user interface and functionality

interpreted language—code that is not compiled; a line-by-line interpretation of code takes place each and every time an interpreted language program is run; tends to run slow

interrupt request 0—*see IRQ 0*

interrupt request 1—*see IRQ 1*

interrupt request 2—*see IRQ 2*

interrupt request 3—*see IRQ 3*

interrupt request 4—*see IRQ 4*

interrupt request 5—*see IRQ 5*

interrupt request 6—*see IRQ 6*

interrupt request 7—*see IRQ 7*

interrupt request 8—*see IRQ 8*

interrupt request 9—*see IRQ 9*

interrupt request 10—*see IRQ 10*

interrupt request 11—*see IRQ 11*

interrupt request 12—*see IRQ 12*

interrupt request 13—*see IRQ 13*

interrupt request 14—*see IRQ 14*

interrupt request 15—*see IRQ 15*

intranet—an organizational network that is used solely within an organization rather than between organizations; internal or private TCP/IP network that provides Internet-type functionality within a LAN or WAN but not connected to the Internet

intrusion detection—tools to detect unauthorized system break-ins

IP—Internet Protocol; basic Internet transmission protocol based on a connectionless best effort packet delivery

IP address—Internet Protocol address; a computer's address that allows it to send and receive mail from other computers on the Internet; a specific 32-bit (four-octet) unique address assigned to each networked device; implemented as 204.222.32.10

IP datagram—Internet Protocol datagram; basic unit of information that passes across the Internet; contains data, source, and destination address information

IPng—Internet Protocol–next generation; term for the next generation of 128-bit (16-byte) IP addressing scheme; *see also IPv6*

IPsec—low-level protocol for encrypting Internet Protocol (IP) packets to provide confidentiality, authentication, and integrity

IPv6—name of the next version of 128-bit IP

IPX—internetwork packet exchange; protocol used in Novell NetWare LANs; *see also IPX/SPX and NWLink*

IPX/SPX—internetwork packet exchange/sequence packet exchange; protocol group used in conjunction with Novell NetWare LANs; *see also IPX and NWLink*

IRM—information resource management; department within a facility that provides data automation, hardware, software, and user support

IRQ 0—interrupt request 0; standard interrupt assignment for the system timer

IRQ 1—interrupt request 1; standard interrupt assignment for the keyboard

IRQ 2—interrupt request 2; standard interrupt assignment for the system I/O, video board

IRQ 3—interrupt request 3; standard interrupt assignment for COM2 and COM 4 serial port(s)

IRQ 4—interrupt request 4; standard interrupt assignment for COM 1 and COM 3 serial port(s)

IRQ 5—interrupt request 5; standard interrupt assignment for LPT2 printer, MIDI device, or network board

IRQ 6—interrupt request 6; standard interrupt assignment for the floppy disk drive

IRQ 7—interrupt request 7; standard interrupt assignment for LPT1 printer

IRQ 8—interrupt request 8; standard interrupt assignment for the real time clock

IRQ 9—interrupt request 9; free interrupt assignment or interrupt assignment for the sound card

IRQ 10—interrupt request 10; free interrupt assignment or interrupt assignment for the primary SCSI adapter/controller

IRQ 11—interrupt request 11; free interrupt assignment or interrupt assignment for the secondary SCSI adapter/controller

IRQ 12—interrupt request 12; standard interrupt assignment for the PS/2 mouse

IRQ 13—interrupt request 13; standard interrupt assignment for the math coprocessor

IRQ 14—interrupt request 14; standard interrupt assignment for the primary hard disk controller

IRQ 15—interrupt request 15; free interrupt assignment or standard interrupt assignment for the secondary hard disk controller

ISA—industry standard architecture; 8- and 16-bit internal bus or used to identify an Internet server application

ISDN—integrated services digital network; a digital telephone network with a channel designed for high-speed voice, video, and data transmission services; international standard for transmitting voice, video, and data to support a wide range of services over the public telephone lines

ISDN basic rate—integrated services digital network basic rate; 2 B + D; high-speed digital network available through telephone carriers where the same paths are used to establish connections for different services; integrates voice and data connections up to 128 Kbps through the use of two 64 K, B-channels in conjunction with one 16 K, D-channel for control and signaling; earmarked to replace existing conventional telephone lines

ISDN primary rate—integrated services digital network primary rate; high-speed digital network available through telephone carriers where the same paths are used to establish connections for different services; integrates voice and data connections through the use of twenty-three 65 K B-channels in conjunction with one 16 K D-channel for control and signaling

ISO—independent sales organization; an organization that serves as an intermediary between a bank and a small merchant and that processes credit card transactions from the merchants

ISP—Internet service provider; company that provides Internet connectivity and Internet-related services; services can consist of hardware, DHCP services, WWW-site hosting, and domain names

ITMRA—Information Technology Management Reform Act of 1996; former name of the Clinger-Cohen Act of 1996

Java—a language for adding interactivity to web pages

John von Neumann Architecture—RAM+ROM+CPU+INPUT+
OUTPUT

Joint Photographic Experts Group—see JPEG

journaling—recording of all computer system activities and uses
of a computer system; used to identify access violations and the
individual accountable for them, determine security exposures,
track the activities of users, and adjust access control measures
when warranted

JPEG—Joint Photographic Experts Group; standard for encoding,
transmitting, and decoding full-color and gray-scale still images

JPEG Compression—a generic algorithm to compress still images

KB—kilobyte; equal to 1024 bytes

Kbps—kilobits per second; transmission of 1000 bits per second

Kennedy-Kassenbaum Bill—*see HIPAA*

Kerberos—network security system for securing higher-level applications, such as distributed environments, that provides confidentiality and authentication without transmitting information over a network that might compromise security

kernel—the core component of an operating system; it is the part of the system that manages files, peripherals, memory, and system resources; it runs the processes and provides communication between the processes

key—an input that controls the transformation of data by an encryption algorithm to protect transmissions in open environments

KHz—kilohertz; one thousand cycles per second

kill—UNIX command to stop a process

kilobyte—1024 bytes

knowledge—the relationships, facts, assumptions, heuristics, and conceptual models derived through formal or informal data interpretation and analysis; knowledge has the attributes of accuracy, relevance, quality, and type; it is used for determining a need, making a decision, and evaluating actions

knowledge acquisition—the process of extracting expertise from humans to be incorporated into a computer program; methods include interviews, computer-based interactive techniques, use of rating and sorting tasks, and protocol analysis

knowledge-based system—*see expert system*

knowledge engineering—a field concerned with the development of various forms of computer-based decision support; this includes both acquisition and structuring of knowledge within a computer system; it includes the process of reducing a large body of knowledge to a precise set of facts and rules

Korn Shell—enhanced interactive UNIX Borne shell developed by David Korn; prompted by $

LAN—local area network; a network of physically interconnected computers that is localized within a small geographical area; operates in a span of short distances (office, building, or complex of buildings)

laser smart card—*see optical card*

last in first out—*see LIFO*

LAT—local area transport; nonroutable but bridgeable protocol used by DEC to support terminal servers; used extensively throughout CHCS

LCD—liquid crystal display; the display screen of an electronic device

leased line—permanent communications link owned by the telephone line but leased for dedicated customer use

legacy systems—usually refers to older mainframe computers that have been in use for a long period of time, contain many years of data, and have been used over many years of software development; also used to describe a system or software application that is a candidate for replacement or migration to some degree of modernization

length of stay—*see ALOS*

LFN—long file name; file name that may be up to 255 characters long; Windows 95 and Windows NT support long file names, MS-DOS does not

license—authorization to use a software product

LIFO—last in first out; a queue that executes last-in requests before previously queued requests; a stack

line editor—*see EDLIN*

line-of-sight—propagation along an unobstructed path

link—a connection between two network devices

LLC—logical link control; upper part of the second layer of the OSI model; oversees and controls the exchange of data between two network nodes

LMHOSTS—text file that maps IP addresses to Windows computer names (NetBIOS names) to network computers outside the local subnet; acts as a local WINS equivalent to provide a static type of WINS service

local area network—*see LAN*

local area network —a network in which all of the computers are connected within a few hundred yards to the same network hub

local area transport—*see LAT*

Localmon.dll—Windows NT print monitor for print jobs delivered to local LPT output

LocalTalk—networking cabling standard used by Macintosh computers; transmits at 230 KB per second over STP at distances up to 300 feet; supports only 32 computers per segment

logic bomb—a program written or modified to produce unexpected results when certain conditions, such as a specified date, are met

logical drive—subdivision of a large physical drive into numerous smaller drives

logical link control—*see LLC*

logical threat—a threat of destruction or alteration of software or data; would be realized by logical manipulation within the system rather than by physical attack

logical unit—*see LU*

login controls—specific conditions users must meet for gaining access to a computer system

logoff—process of closing an open server session

logon—process of opening a server session through authentication

logon process—the interaction between a user and the computer system that enables the user to utilize the computer system

long file name—*see LFN*

longitudinal data—data set that follows individuals over time; data that describe a specific group of people who are observed over a period of time; *see also cohort data*

longitudinal/lifetime patient record—*see longitudinal patient record*

longitudinal patient record—a patient record that is structured to include the documentation of care provided from all past sites of care during a given period, versus keeping separate records at each primary care site or hospitalization location with no ability for centralized access of the medical information; the growth of automation to support medicine has brought a focus toward longitudinal records within networks or local systems of care; *see also CPR*

loophole—incomplete code or an error in a computer program or in the hardware, which permits circumvention of the access control mechanism

LOS—length of stay; *see also ALOS*

lossless compression—compression algorithm that provides total recovery of all the data in a compressed file when it is uncompressed; provides a compression ratio of 2:1

lossy compression—compression algorithm that permits an acceptable loss of data when a compressed file is uncompressed; provides a compression ratio of 100:1 to 200:1

Lprmon.dll—Windows NT print monitor for print jobs delivered to UNIX-based printers

LTC—long-term care; also called continuing care; this segment of rapidly growing information systems products assists the health care continuum that consists of maintenance, custodial, and health services for the chronically ill, disabled, or those patients requiring medical or social day care; may be provided on an inpatient (rehabilitation facility, nursing home, skilled nursing facility, mental hospital) or outpatient basis, or at home

LU—logical unit; portion of the ALU within the CPU that coordinates logical operations

M

MAC—media access control; lower portion of the second layer of the OSI model; identifies the actual physical link between two nodes

MAC address—media access control address; synonym for unique hardware physical address of a network device identified at the media access control layer and stored in ROM

magnetic stripe card—a smart card containing a magnetic stripe that can store about 800 bits (100 bytes) of information; largely used as banking cards and for security access applications

mailslots—connection oriented interprocess messaging interface between clients and servers in a Windows NT environment (impersonation)

mainframe—large scale computer capable of supporting many users and peripherals

MAN—metropolitan area network; provides high-speed data transfer regional connectivity through multiple physical networks; operates over distances sufficient for a metropolitan area; IEEE 802.6 standard

management information department—*see MID*

management information system—*see MIS*

masquerading—obtaining proper identification through improper means (such as wiretapping) and then accessing a system as a legitimate user

master browser—computer on a network that maintains a list of all computers and services available on the network

Master CNE—*see MCNE*

master person index—*see MPI*

math coprocessor—accompanying integrated chip to the CPU that performs arithmetic functions, which allows the CPU to perform system functions

MAU—multiple station access unit; token-ring network hub

Mb—Megabit; 1,048,576 bits or 1024 KB

MB—megabyte; one million bytes

Mbps—Megabits per second; transmission of one million bits per second

MCNE—Master Certified Network Engineer; a network engineering certification that is a distinctive accomplishment requiring skills above that of a CNE; *see also CNE*

MCP—Microsoft Certified Professional; operating system–level Microsoft certification; MCPs provide day-to-day resource administration, operating system implementation, tuning, and integration on Windows operating systems

MCSE—Microsoft Certified Systems Engineer; systems-level Microsoft certification; MCSEs provide systems engineering, implementation, tuning, integration, and networking engineering on Windows NT systems

MCT—Microsoft Certified Trainer; MCTs teach Windows NT concepts and are NT technical resources

MDI-X port—hub port that can be configured to provide a crossover function that reverses the transmit and receive wire pairs; used to daisy chain hubs together with a standard drop cable; alleviates creating a crossover cable to perform the same function

mean time between failure—*see MTBF*

mean time to diagnose—*see MTTD*

mean time to repair—*see MTTR*

media access control—*see MAC*

media access control address—*see MAC address*

medical cognition—the field of study concerned with understanding the cognitive processes, such as reasoning, decision making, and problem solving in medical practice

medical expert system—an expert system that aids physicians or other medical providers in solving complex medical problems; *see also expert system*

medical imaging—the field concerned with the study and use of digital or analog images generated to view structures or processes within a human body; images are often produced by radiographic methods

Medicare Part A—an insurance program (also called Hospital Insurance Program) that provides basic protection against the costs of hospital and related posthospital services for: individuals age 65 or over and eligible for retirement benefits under the Social Security or the Railroad Retirement System, individuals under age 65 entitled for not less than 24 months to benefits under the Social Security or Railroad Retirement System on the basis of disability, and certain other individuals with end-stage renal disease and covered by the Social Security or Railroad Retirement System; after various cost-sharing requirements are met, Part A pays for inpatient hospital, skilled nursing facility (SNF), and home health care; the Hospital Insurance Program is financed from a separate trust fund, primarily funded with a payroll tax levied on employers, employees, and the self-employed; *see also Medicare*

Medicare Part B—supplementary Medical Insurance Program, which is a voluntary portion of Medicare, and includes physician's services to all enrollees who are willing to pay a monthly premium, and are also entitled to Medicare Part A

MEDS—minimum emergency data set; a standardized view of the critical components of a patient's medical history

megahertz—*see MHz*

member category or member type—one of a group of classification breakdowns by either age groups for pediatric or adult, or the eligibility to receive Medicare, which is tied to the structure that determines physician pay

member enrollment—this module with a managed care information system must handle a variety of functions, such as who is enrolled, the patient transaction history, and the patient's multiple assignment

member month—the count that includes member counts and retro (retroactive) adds and deletes, resulting in one month in which one member is enrolled

member server—nondomain Windows NT server that provides file, print, or application services

members per year—the basic measure of the number of annualized members enrolled in a health plan; total member months divided by 12 months

memory—area of a computer used to store data; can be RAM or ROM; *see RAM and also ROM*

menu interaction—a type of interface in which the user can choose from among a list of possible choices or menus

merchant status—term used to indicate a business is authorized to accept credit cards in payment for goods and services

metadata—data concerning the structure of data in a database stored in the data dictionary; metadata are used to describe information such as the structure of tables, columns, constraints, and indexes; *see application metadata*

metropolitan area network—a backbone network that covers a metropolitan area and is regulated by state or local utility commissions; suppliers that provide MAN services are telephone companies and cable services; they are used by companies that need networks that span public rights-of-way

MFM—modified frequency modulation; data recording technique used on hard drives associated with AT computers

MHz—megahertz; one million times per second; measurement of CPU speed

Micro Channel—Micro Channel Architecture; IBM 32-bit multi-processing system and interface hardware bus standard for PS/2 computers

microcomputer—desktop or laptop/notebook computer employing a microprocessor

microprocessor—central processing unit; *see also CPU*

microsecond—one-millionth of a second

Microsoft Certified Professional—*see MCP*

Microsoft Certified Systems Engineer—*see MCSE*

Microsoft Certified Trainer—*see MCT*

Microsoft Challenge Handshake Protocol—*see MS-CHAP*

Microsoft Disk Operating System—*see MS-DOS*

microwave—high-frequency radio waves used for point-to-point communication of audio, video, and data signals, with a spectrum generally above two gigahertz (GHz)

MID—management information department; department within a facility that provides data automation, hardware, software, and user support

migration system—an existing or planned automated information system or application that has been designated as the replacement for a legacy system; *see also legacy system*

Migration Tool for NetWare—utility included in Windows NT to migrate NetWare user accounts, group accounts, files, and directories from a NetWare server environment to a Windows NT server environment; GSNW and NWLink must be installed before a migration can take place

millions of instructions per second—*see MIPS*

millisecond—one-thousandth of a second

MIME—see Multipurpose Internet Mail Extensions

minicomputer—small to medium scale computer that often uses dumb terminals

MIPS—millions of instructions per second; rate that a processor executes instructions; used as a measurement of processing power and computer speed

MIS—management information system; a system to provide information to support operations, management, analysis, and decision-making functions within an organization; it involves the use of computer hardware and software, data and database, manual procedures, models for analysis, planning, control, and decision making

mirror set—RAID level 1; two-disk array where one disk shadows the contents of the original disk to maintain instant redundancy

miscellaneous expense—expense connected with hospital insurance; hospital charges other than room and board, such as X-rays, drugs, laboratory fees, and other ancillary charges

mission critical system—the designation of a system as being the most vital to the core business operation in a way that warrants special consideration, protection, or backup provisions to prevent against fire, vandalism, natural disaster, or system failure as part of either a century date strategy or disaster plan

modem—modulator/demodulator; device that converts digital data to analog signals for transmission over a telephone line and performs analog to digital signals conversion for the receiving node

modified frequency modulation—*see MFM*

module—a subelement of a software program

motherboard—main system board of the computer that consists of the CPU, I/O bus, and built-in peripherals

Motion Picture Experts Group—*see MPEG*

mouse—desktop input device used with GUI systems providing cursor control and program execution features; when the mouse is moved across a desktop in a particular direction and distance, it causes a relational movement of the cursor on the computer screen

MPEG—Motion Picture Experts Group; standard for digital encoding, transmitting, decoding, and presentation of VCR-quality motion video

MPI—master patient index or master person index; a central patient identification and storage segment that is becoming a popular and necessary component for today's management of a patient's clinical and associated financial information; this index links with, or stores directly, the patient-related data elements selected by users within a system or community; popular data elements include: name, social security number, primary physician identification, medication or allergy lists, and insurance benefits, together with a large number of locally selected options

MSAU—multiple station access unit; token-ring network hub

MS-CHAP—Microsoft Challenge Handshake Protocol; Windows NT password authentication and data encryption method that uses the RSA Data Security MD4 (Message Digest Four) algorithm; used in conjunction with the remote access server (RAS) for dial-in connections to a Windows NT Server

MS-DOS—Microsoft Disk Operating System; set of 16-bit software programs that direct system-level computer operation; developed by Microsoft in the early 1980s for the 8086 CPU

MTBF—mean time between failure; device operating time before a failure occurs

MTBF—mean time before failure; operation time before a product is expected to fail

MTTD—mean time to diagnose; time it takes to diagnose a problem

MTTR—mean time to repair; time to restore a device to service from a failure

multicast—network transmission meant for multiple, but not all network, nodes; technique that allows copies of a single packet to be passed to a select number of nodes within a subnet

multi-homed host—computer that is physically connected to two networks; has two IP addresses assigned to it; one for each network interface

multimedia—communications that combine voice, video, and graphics that require large amounts of disk space for storage and large amounts of bandwidth for transmission

multiple master domain—Windows NT master network domain for large networks with multiple administration domains for accounts; maintains trusts to resource domains administered by those domains

multiple station access unit—*see MAU, MSAU, and SMAU*

multiplexer—device that enables a single digital communications channel to carry data transmission from multiple voice or data sources simultaneously; reduces the cost of data transmissions by merging data into one line; *see also MUX*

multiplexor—*see MUX*

multiprocessing—capability of a computer with two or more CPUs to execute multiple processes across CPUs

Multipurpose Internet Mail Extensions (MIME)—an Internet standard to provide different types of data, such as audio, video, graphics, and text in electronic mail messages

multitasking—ability of an operating system to run multiple tasks concurrently; Windows NT and OS/2 are multitasking operating systems

MUX—multiplexer or multiplexor; network device where multiple streams of information are combined from different sources onto a common medium for transmission

named pipes—one- or two-way pipe used for connectionless interprocess messaging interface between clients and servers

NAT—network address translation

National Practitioner Data Bank—*see NPDB*

National Provider Identifier—*see NPI*

NDIS—Network Driver Interface Specification; for writing device drivers for network interface cards using the NDIS specification, multiple protocols can be bound to a single network adapter

NDSS—Nursing Decision Support System; automated system designed to reproduce the expert skill of the nurse; NDSSs differ from other information systems in that they are designed to emulate the specific human cognitive and reasoning processes used in nursing decisions

need-to-know—the access authorization or the specification of the kind of data to be made available to an authorized user or an authorized computer system

NetBEUI—NetBIOS Extended User Interface; fast, easy to install, nonconfigurable, nonroutable network protocol for use with up to 200 network nodes; resides at the OSI transport layer

NetBIOS Extended User Interface—*see NetBEUI*

NetBIOS—Network Basic Input Output System; standard interface to networks employing IBM and compatible PCs; implemented at the application layer; NetBIOS names cannot exceed 15 characters

net loss ratio—HMOs calculate this ratio of claims and miscellaneous expenses, over premium revenues; the ratio includes accounting for all expenses, versus the medical loss ratio cost of only medical claim expenses; *see also medical loss ratio*

Netscape Navigator—a component within a suite of Internet tools called Netscape communicator; a web browser

NetWare—Novell's network operating system for PCs; uses the IPX/SPX network protocol; NetWare 2.2 is a 16-bit operating system; NetWare 3.X and 4.X are 32-bit operating systems

network—series of networks and nodes connected by communications channels

network adapter card—computer hardware adapter card that provides an interface between a computer and the network

Network Basic Input Output System—*see NetBIOS*

network drive—shared disk drive available to network users

Network Driver Interface Specification—*see NDIS*

Network Information Center—*see InterNIC*

network interface card—*see NIC*

network layer—third layer of the OSI model; routes data from source to destination across networks and handles addressing and switching; the network layer performs network communications at the most basic level sending frames on the media, and examining and receiving frames that match its address; also, the network layer establishes and manages the connections through which data are transferred; also known as the Internet layer

network operating system—see NOS

network printer—shared printer available to network users; can be connected to a print server, directly connected to the network, or shared from a workstation

network redirector—operating system feature that intercepts requests from the computer and directs them to the local or remote machine for processing; resides at the OSI presentation layer

network supervisor access level—individual who has access to all functions, including security

network traffic—data transmitted on a network for the purpose of sending information from one node to another or from one network to another

New Technology—*see NT*

New Technology File System—*see NTFS*

nibble—first or last half of an eight-bit byte; a half byte

NIC—network interface card or Network Information Center; mainly synonymous with network interface cards

NIST—National Institute of Standards and Technology

node—computer or device connected to a network that is also called a host

nonoverwriting virus—appends the virus code to the physical end of a program, or moves the original code to another location

nonrepudiation—cryptographic receipts which ensure that the author of a message cannot falsely deny sending the message; proof that only the signer could have created a signature; a basis of legal recognition of electronic signatures

nonroutable protocols—*see NetBEUI, LAT, and DLC*

nonvolatile memory—memory that retains its content when power is removed

NOS—network operating system; operating system used on network servers to provide file, print, and other services to clients; includes Windows NT Server, Novell NetWare, Banyan Vines (on top of UNIX), IBM OS/2 LAN Server, and OpenVMS

NOT—logical gating operation that provides a low output if an input is high; provides a high output if an input is low

NPDB—National Practitioner Data Bank; an entity with a database that is a resource for previous physician discipline or malpractice payment experience; mandatory for query by HMOs and also sought by private and federal hospitals or health systems, and even required for query by some state laws; an early step toward credentialing a provider for clinical privileges or granting status as medical director or medical staff positions; requery of NPDB is required at a two-year interval for reappointment

NPI—National Provider Identifier; part of the administrative simplification provision of HIPAA Title XI, Part C of the Social Security Act; a standardized provider number proposed for future use by the Department of Health and Human Services, consisting of an 8-byte alphanumeric identifier, with no embedded intelligence, and the eighth digit serving as a check digit; numbers would be maintained by the Health Care Financing Administration; optional policy includes centralized government registry and listings and issuances by a combination of federal and Medicaid state agencies

NT—New Technology; short name for Microsoft's Windows NT operating system; *see also Windows NT server*

NTDETECT.COM—Windows NT operating system boot process file that detects hardware installed in a machine and updates the registry with this information

NTFS—New Technology File System; secure transaction-oriented file system used with Windows NT to manage disk space and provides, among other features, user authentication, directory and file level security, and fault tolerance

NTLDR—Windows NT operating system boot process file that initiates and executes the boot process

null modem cable—serial cable with transmit and receive pins crossed to simulate a modem for a direct connection between computers

nurse hotline or triage system—a type of telephone triage system that assists nurses in positions of responsibility to receive patient calls, document their concerns or symptoms, and use a decision-tree algorithm to determine the urgency of the patient's need to be seen by a physician; these system's feature easy documentation and retrieval, and protection against medical-legal lawsuits due to the accuracy and availability of documented discussions; *see also telephone triage system*

Nursing Decision Support System—*see NDSS*

nursing informatics—the use of any computer and information technologies that support any nursing function carried out by nurses in the performance of their duties

NWLink—NetWare Link protocol; Microsoft's implementation of the IPX/SPX protocol; can be used as the network protocol in a Windows NT network; must be used in conjunction with GSNW when connecting to NetWare servers from a Windows NT server

object—a block of information that has additional information that describes the data, the application that created it, how to format it, and the location of related information stored in a separate file; may be a block of information from a spreadsheet or a graphic from a drawing

object code—the machine code generated by a source code language processor, such as an assembler or compiler; a file of object code may be immediately executable or it may require linking with other object code files, such as libraries, to produce a complete executable program

object oriented programming—an approach to software development that combines data and procedures into a single object or package of data; this method of programming allows designers to create rapid and highly flexible systems that allow existing object modules to be incorporated into new programs rather than having to completely rewrite new modules of computer code

object request broker—the common interface that permits object-to-object communication across mixed-vendor environments

object reuse—computer code in existing objects is reused to create new objects

OC-1—Optical Carrier 1; 51 Mbps rate of transmission over optical fiber

OC-3—Optical Carrier 3; 155 Mbps rate of transmission over optical fiber

OC-12—Optical Carrier 12; 622 Mbps rate of transmission over optical fiber

OC-48—Optical Carrier 48; 2.488 Mbps rate of transmission over optical fiber

octal—base-eight numbering system where three bits are used to represent each digit; uses the 0–7 digits for representations

octet—eight-bit or one byte unit of data; four octets are used in an IP address

odd parity—method of data parity that uses an odd number of "1" bits in each byte or word; the parity bit is set for an odd number of 1 bits

OEM—original equipment manufacturer

office visit—the cognitive primary care office setting that involves examination of, or education and discussion with, the patient; also used to define the event or setting for the provision of medical services other than physician services; arguably an underpaid health care setting that was the focus of RBRVS (resource-based relative value scale) in attempting to achieve a better equality between the office visit and other procedural, surgical, or diagnostic services

offline—device not available to be connected to or controlled by a computer

OLTP—*see on-line transaction processing*

on-chip applications—applications that reside on an integrated circuit chip

online—device available to be connected to or controlled by a computer

on-line transaction processing—process in which transactions are executed immediately, rather than batched and then executed later; examples are bank ATM transaction and airline reservations

OOA—out-of-area; the treatment obtained by a covered person outside the network service area, as defined in the contract; an area (where health care services or supplies may be received) outside the region defined by the HMO as its service area, where only emergency services are allowed; *see also in-area*

OOP—out-of-pocket; the cost of health treatment or services that must be paid by the patient, which includes coinsurance, copayment, and deductible amounts; *see deductible*

OP—outpatient; a person who receives health care services without being admitted to a hospital

open card system—a smart card system that allows the cards to be used at any bank or business that accepts cards for payment; *see also closed card system*

open shortest path first—*see OSPF*

open system—*see open systems architecture*

open systems architecture—use of standardized technology and structure for hardware, operating system, databases, fault tolerances, and networking and communications transport; an important element of medical information systems design, which allows an organization to develop or add to systems that have been selected for their compatibility with a wide variety of other instruments or technology; a valuable consideration for member services or customer service operations; precludes spending money on systems that are not compatible with future expansion requirements

open systems environment—software systems that can operate on different hardware platforms because they use components that follow the same standards for user interfaces, applications, and network protocols

Open Systems Interconnection—*see OSI*

operating system—software that manages basic computer operations; *see also Windows NT, OS/2, and UNIX*

Operating System 2—*see OS/2 or WARP*

operating system certification—a guarantee that no design and/ or implementation flaw is present in the operating system and that the occurrence of a random hardware and/or software error is below a specified value

Operating System Interface Layer—the layer that allows for the interconnection and interrelationship among the various operating systems in the form of two or more devices, applications, and the user interfacing with an application or device

optical card—an optical memory card with laser-recorded and laser-read information that can be edited or updated and has a storage capacity of 800 printed pages; data are stored by engraving microscopic pits onto the optical layer of the card surface, and the data cannot be erased; also called a laser smart card

Optical Carrier 1—*see OC-1*

Optical Carrier 3—*see OC-3*

Optical Carrier 12—*see OC-12*

Optical Carrier 48—*see OC-48*

OR—logical gating operation that provides a high output if any input is high

ORB—*see object request broker*

OS/2—Operating System 2; IBM's 32-bit GUI multitasking operating system with the ability to run DOS, Win16, Win32, OS/2 16, and OS/2 32 applications for 80286 and 80386 computers; *see WARP*

OSI—Open Systems Interconnection; reference model to the protocols in the seven-layer data communications networking standards model and the services performed at each level; the OSI standard is defined by the International Standards Organization (ISO); the seven layers are: physical, data link, network, transport, session, presentation, and application

OSPF—open shortest path first; routing protocol that routes across multiple possible paths; a link state routing protocol

outcome—also called health outcome, or the result of a process of prevention, detection, or treatment; an indicator of the effectiveness of health care measures upon patients

outcomes measurement—a method of systematically monitoring a patient's medical or surgical intervention or nonintervention together with the associated responses, including measures of morbidity and functional status; findings from outcomes studies enable managed care entities to outline protocols according to their findings

out-of-network—may consist of hospital care or other provider services that are rendered by nonparticipating provider entities, due to the purposeful selection by the enrollee or the occurrence of an illness or injury while on out-of-area travel; some plans call for the member to pay the fees, while others allow for coverage under a higher copay by the member

out-of-plan referral—referrals to specialists who are not participating providers, which must be preauthorized by the system of plan medical director

out-of-pocket costs—*see OOP*

out-of-pocket limit—a stated limitation of out-of-pocket costs, which provides a comfort or guarantee to the patient that all costs will be provided, once the limit is reached for health services received during the contract year for all care except that which is outlined as excluded for coverage

overwriting virus—will destroy code or data in the host program by replacing it with the virus code

ownership—a patient's medical record is maintained and owned by a health care provider; this practice is established by statutes and licensing regulations in many states, which grant the provider control over the physical document, but give the patient ownership-type rights to the information contained in the record—the patient generally has control over the release of patient-identifiable (confidential) information, except in circumstances identified by case law, by federal or state statutes and regulations, and by provider policy

P6—Pentium 686; development name of the Pentium Pro computer

packet—any small block of specifically characterized data sent over a packet switching network

packet-filtering firewall—a computer that evaluates data, packet-by-packet, to determine if a packet should be copied from one network to another

packet format—contains three sections: the header, data, and trailer

packet header—first three octets of an X.25 packet that specifies packet destination, source, and contains an alert

Packet Internet Groper—*see PING*

packet sniffing—a technique in which attackers surreptitiously insert a software program at remote network switches or hot computers; the program monitors information packets as they are sent through networks and sends a copy of the information retrieved to the hacker; by picking up the first 125 keystrokes of a connection, attackers can learn passwords and user identifications, which, in turn, they can use to break into systems

packet switched network—a network that supports packet switching, and exchanges messages between different computers by sending a message in a number of uniformly sized packets along common channels, shared with other computers, as opposed to using a dedicated circuit; *see also packet switching*

packet switching—transmission technique in which data are broken up into packets and sent along multiple destination paths using store and forward techniques

PACS—picture archiving and communication systems; widely used to manage clinical image data, primarily in radiology, and to provide timely access to referring physicians both within the institution and at remote sites

PAP—password authentication protocol; allows the use of clear text passwords at its lowest level

parallel processing—the simultaneous use of more than one computer to solve a problem, or the simultaneous use of a single computer's processor to solve simultaneous operations

Passive Star Topology Network—star topology configured with a box that organizes the wiring; *see Active Star Topology*

passive threat—a potential breach of security, which would not change the state of a system; if it occurred the threat could arise from unauthorized reading of files or use of the computer system for an unauthorized application

password—a special code word, or a string of characters, that a user must present before gaining access to a data system's resources; a sequence of characters that an individual presents to a system for purposes of authentication

password authentication protocol—*see PAP*

password cracking—a technique in which attackers try to guess or steal passwords to obtain access to computer systems

patient care information system—*see PCIS*

patient sensitive (deniable) information—sensitive information, and often having medical-legal implications, that is available only through security access rules to only those individuals with a bona fide need to know (e.g., adoption information, HIV test results and treatment, substance abuse, suspected rape)

patient telemanagement—the periodic follow-up of a patient by telephone; the goal is to avoid an undetected or uncommunicated patient need, which may become aggravated to the point of requiring more expensive intervention, or an office visit; may be performed by various skill levels, depending upon the patient need: physician, nurse, technician, or even a volunteer; often telemanagement involves questions to chronically ill or elderly patients that help to ensure compliance in taking medication properly, or to detect weight gain or loss; remarkable savings have resulted from telemanagement

PC card slot—the port in a computer in which a smart card is inserted via a 68-pin socket connector; available in types I, II, and III form factors; types I and II measure 2.25 inches x 3.5 inches x .25 inches, and type III measures 2.25 inches x 3.5 inches x .375 inches; the type II form factor is the most prevalent

PCI—peripheral component interconnect; standard CPU to I/O device interface with 32, 64, and 128 bit data paths; PCI motherboards automatically configure interrupts; introduced in 1993

PCIS—patient care information system; patient care-related applications that are generally part of a hospital information system

PCMCIA—Personal Computer Memory Card International Association; association that has worked to standardize and promote PC card technology

PDC—primary domain controller; first operational computer in a Windows NT domain and only PDC in a domain; authenticates all users and maintains the master security accounts database

pediatric hotline or triage system—one type of specialized telephone triage system for pediatric application; pediatric practices may choose to install a telephone system to either reduce the evening and weekend call demands for their practice, or to reduce unnecessary office visits; some practices that have only a small portion of their revenue derived from capitation have actually seen office visits fall to the point of negatively impacted revenue beyond a desired outcome; see also *telephone triage system*

peer-to-peer network—LAN with no central computer where 10 or fewer user computers are connected together, and share the use of devices on an equal basis; also called a workgroup

penetration—a successful and unauthorized access to privileged (i.e., clinical) data from a protected database or system

Pentium—fifth generation Intel microprocessor that employs a 64-bit internal bus and 64-bit external bus; used in IBM compatible computers; operates at speeds of 90 MHz–133 MHz; capable of over 100 MIPS

Pentium II—Intel microprocessor that employs a 300-bit internal bus, 64-bit external bus, a dual independent 64-bit cache, and 64-bit system bus; used in IBM compatible computers; operates at speeds of 233, 266, 300, and 333 MHz

Pentium 686—*see P6 and Pentium Pro*

Pentium Pro—sixth generation Intel microprocessor that employs a 300-bit internal bus, 64-bit external bus, dual independent 64-bit cache, and 64-bit system bus; used in IBM compatible computers; operates at speeds of 150 MHz or higher; capable of over 300 MIPS; optimized for 32-bit software

peripheral component interconnect—*see PCI*

peripheral device—in a data processing system, any piece of equipment that is distinct from the central processing unit (CPU) that may provide the system with outside communication or additional facilities; *see also CPU*

permanent virtual circuit—*see PVC*

personal computer—a computer workstation that decentralizes computing power to a person's desktop by positioning computer resources in the user's computer rather than in a centralized mainframe computer; *see workstation*

Personal System 2—*see PS/2*

personally identifiable health information—health information that contains an individual's identifiers (e.g., name, social security number, birth date) or contains a sufficient number of variables to allow identification of an individual

PGP—*see pretty good privacy*

physical access—the ability and the means to approach and use any hardware component of a clinical data system

physical layer—first layer in the OSI model; defines the physical characteristics of a link between communicating devices; the physical layer deals with the physical characteristics of how data signals are transmitted on the network, including how the information bits are transmitted and received; cable and/or wire are included in this layer

physical security—the measures taken against all physical threats to a clinical data system, including its remote facilities and operational area (including control of access and exit, protection against fire, explosion, natural disaster, sabotage, social protests, and power problems), and protection of all the stored clinical data from malicious destruction or theft

physician online directory—a type of physician referral service that can be accessed from a computer, through a variety of on-line services; on-line directories can provide printable details of the physician services, medical capabilities, office address and map of the location, and patient access information; most on-line directories provide one-way information to the patient, but some provide interactive two-communication features; directories may be sponsored by any medical group, provider, or health plan wishing to add this recruitment service; *see also physician referral service*

physician referral service—a "yellow pages" written directory service, telephonic service, or Internet listing that assists patients in selecting a physician, based on the needs of the patient; also called physician hotlines, doctors referral line, or physician exchange or guide; the goal of the service is to recruit patients to a medical group, hospital, or health plan that pays for the referral service, or to convert patients from existing relationships with another medical group, hospital, or health plan; often the sponsor of the physician referral service is masked, to minimize the appearance of steering patients; if a provider or medical group does not receive the coverage desired from an insurer, they can create their own service

picosecond—one-trillionth of a second

picture archiving and communication systems—*see PACS*

piggybacking—unauthorized access to information in a computer system by entering a computer program after a user has already logged on but has not logged off before stepping away from the computer; using an authorized person's access code

PIN—personal identification number; used to authenticate or identify a user

PING—Packet InterNet Groper; utility used to test destination reachability; sends an ICMP echo request to the destination and waits for a reply

PIP—periodic interim payment; an advance payment transaction from a payer to a provider that represents some portion of the lag factor for services rendered within an IBNR context; the recent trend is for payers to decrease or eliminate PIPs, based on their clout, which impacts the provider's financial statements in many ways, such as increased accounts receivable; *see also IBNR*

pixel—the smallest unit of data for defining an image in the computer; the computer reduces a picture to a grid of pixels; the term comes from "picture element"

Pjlmon.dll—Windows NT print monitor for print jobs delivered to PJL language printers

PKI—*see public key infrastructure*

PKZip—disk compression program

plain old telephone system—*see POTS and PSTN*

plain text—the original communication form, also called clear text or readable text

platform for Internet content selection—a system for labeling the contents of documents on the World Wide Web; used to censor web sites

plenum cable—fire-resistant cable that is installed in false ceilings; uses a coating that will not emit toxic fumes in the event of a fire

plotter—output device that produces graphs and diagrams

POCS—*see point of care system*

Point of care system—an increasingly popular description for many types of medical information applications or features that provide support for the many decentralized points of care across the care continuum; features may include charting automation for documentation, and subsequent retrieval of patient care information; an open architecture aids the integration with other hospital systems; support can include features for admissions, dietary, chaplains, skilled nursing, ancillary departments of lab and pharmacy, infusion services, hospice, home health, speech therapy, medical social workers, and physical or occupational therapy; *see also CPR*

point-to-multipoint connection—a communications architecture in which multiple devices are connected to a link that branches from a single point called an intelligent controller, which manages the flow of information

point-to-point connection—a communications link between two specific end devices, such as two computers or two modems

Point-to-Point Protocol—*see PPP*

Point-to-Point Tunneling Protocol—*see PPTP*

pop—to remove data from the top of a stack

pop-down list box—in a graphical user interface (GUI) environment, the list box that appears when the user selects an icon that represents a box with various choices

population at risk—a group of individuals subject to, or likely to be subject to, a disease or health problem; the magnitude of the health phenomenon can be measured in numbers of new cases (incidence), number of existing cases (prevalence) that are known as morbidity rates, and general or cause-specific death rates, known as mortality statistics

portable information carrier—a portable device, such as a credit card, that contains one or more technologies used to store information related to an individual and is used in one or more applications; it may contain both updateable and static technologies, such as an integrated circuit chip, magnetic stripe, bar code, and printed media

Portable Open Systems Interface—*see POSIX*

POSIX—Portable Open Systems Interface; IEEE standard for UNIX-like program implementation; capable of case sensitive file naming, last access time stamping, and hard links; a standard, not an operating system; Windows NT supports POSIX

POTS—plain old telephone system; regular dial-up telephone lines; also known as public switched telephone network (PSTN)

Power PC—RISC microprocessor developed by IBM with built-in features that allow it to emulate other microprocessors

PPP—Point-to-Point Protocol; protocol that links two networks for serial data transfer; supports multiple network protocols (TCP/IP, IPX/SPX, and NetBEUI) compression and encryption

PPTP—Point-to-Point Tunneling Protocol; protocol for data transfer over the Internet supporting secure communication through encryption

preemptive multitasking—multitasking operating system technique where the operating system controls application access to the processor

Presentation layer—sixth layer of the OSI model; provides services to interface applications to the communications system in the form of encryption, compression, expansion, translation, and conversion; the network redirector resides here; the presentation layer encodes the application layer requests into the appropriate form for the session layer and vice versa; the presentation layer translates data to ensure that the node is communicating with the network in understandable terms

pretty good privacy—a public key encryption program; used with electronic mail system

primary domain controller—*see PDC*

primary patient record—primary record of care; the primary legal record documenting the health care services provided to a person during health care delivery; this term is synonymous with medical record, or health record; when stored in a computer system and used by caregivers while providing patient care services

primary rate integration—a process of organizing systems in such a way that they provide increased value to the user over the information derived from stand-alone or separate systems; two or more software applications that run on the same physical processor and under the same operating system

printer pool—Windows NT print option that allows a pool of printers to be configured as one; allows jobs sent to the pool to be printed at any one of a number of printers in the pool at a designated printer pool location

print server—a computer that manages print requests from many different users by holding them in a queue until they can be printed; it sends print requests to the appropriate printer in a multiprinter environment

privacy—the right of individuals to keep information about themselves from being disclosed to others; the claim of individuals to be left alone, free from surveillance or interference from other individuals, organizations, or the government

Privacy Act of 1974—prohibits federal agencies, including federal hospitals, from disclosing information contained in a system of records to any person or agency without the written consent of the individual to whom the information pertains; it stipulates that federal agencies must meet certain requirements for the handling of confidential information; it grants people certain rights to information collected about them by the federal government and its agencies; these rights include finding out what information has been collected, to see and have a copy of the information, to correct or amend the information, and to exercise limited control of the disclosure of that information to other parties

private key—a key in an asymmetric algorithm; the possession of this key is restricted, usually to one person or organization

private key cryptography—encryption methodology in which the encryptor and decryptor use the same key, which must be kept secret

privilege—an individual's right to hold private and confidential the information given to a health care provider in a professional relationship; the individual may consent or waive the right to privilege; for example, if a patient brings a lawsuit against a provider and the records are needed to present the provider's case, the privilege is waived

privileged information—a datum or data combination for which adequate technological and administrative safeguards for handling, disclosure, storage, and disposal are required by law or by administrative policy

program—a series of statements or instructions to a computer that tell it how to process data and how to operate

programmable read-only memory—*see PROM*

programmers—technical specialists who write computer software instructions or programs

program security controls—controls which are used to prevent unauthorized changes to programs in systems that are already in production

PROM—programmable read-only memory; subclass of ROM chip used in control devices because it can be programmed once; nonvolatile memory chip with a factory-loaded permanent program

protocol—a set of rules and procedures that govern the format, control, and transmission of data between two or more processes or components in a network

protocol stack—a set of combined protocols that accomplish the communications process

prototyping—a methodology or iterative process whereby a model of a system is quickly developed and continuously modified until it meets all of the requirements of the user

PS/2—Personal System 2; second-generation series of IBM computers that used Micro Channel Architecture

PSTN—public switched telephone network; regular dial-up telephone lines; also known as plain old telephone system (POTS)

public information—data which do not require specific handling, limited disclosure, protected storage, and disposal

public key—a key in an asymmetric algorithm that is widely available and is used to encode messages; used for verifying a signature after it has been signed; *see digital signature*

public key algorithms—a method of cryptography in which one key is used to encrypt a message and another key is used to decrypt it; the encryption key is called the "public key" because it can be made widely available without compromising the secrecy of the message or the decryption key; the decryption key is called the "private key" or "secret key"

public key cryptography—encryption system that uses a linked pair of keys; one key encrypts, the other key decrypts; can be used for creating digital signatures

public key infrastructure—technology, facilities, people, operational procedures, and policy to support public key-based security mechanisms; it is an enabler for these encryption and digital signatures

public switched telephone network—*see PSTN*

push—putting data on a stack

PVC—permanent virtual circuit; fixed circuit between two users in a packet-switched network

queue—FIFO waiting area for processing; *see also FIFO*

QWERTY—the keyboard layout named after the first six letters on the top left row of keys

radio-frequency interference—a disruption caused by radio and television; a subset of electromagnetic interference

RAID—redundant array of inexpensive (independent) disks; interconnected disks that share the responsibility for storage of data

RAID 0—redundant array of inexpensive (independent) disks level 0; striping without parity; storage technique that "stripes" data in 64 K blocks across all disks in the array; a minimum of two disks is required for RAID 0

RAID 1—redundant array of inexpensive (independent) disks level 1; *see disk mirroring*

RAID 3—redundant array of inexpensive (independent) disks level 3; striping with parity; fault tolerant storage technique that "stripes" data in 64 K blocks across all disks in the array; maintains a separate disk for parity information; a minimum of three disks is required for RAID 3 striping with parity

RAID 5—redundant array of inexpensive (independent) disks level 5; striping with parity; fault-tolerant storage technique that "stripes" data and parity information in 64 K blocks across all disks in the array; a minimum of three disks is required for RAID 5 striping with parity

RAM—random access memory; read-write volatile memory where data are stored for manipulation by the CPU; storage attribute is lost if power is interrupted; primary storage of data or program instructions that can directly access any randomly chosen location in the same amount of time

random access memory—*see RAM*

RARP—Reverse Address Resolution Protocol; discovers the IP address of a device by broadcasting a request on a network; hardware address to IP address resolution

RAS—remote access server; dial-in capability of Windows NT providing remote access to the server or the entire network from a remote location; allows the use of modems, ISDN, and X.25 adapters for connectivity

RDISK—Windows NT command to initiate the creation or updating of an emergency repair disk; *see also ERD*

read-only memory—*see ROM*

reader/writer—a smart card reader/writer device that provides a means for passing information from a smart card to a larger computer and for writing information from the larger computer onto a smart card; physically links the card's hardware interface to the larger computer

reader/writer driver layer—the layer in various reader and writer devices that pulls information from, writes to, or erases segments and/or zones of a smart card

real-time system—on-line computer that generates a nearly simultaneous output from the inputs received

reasonable charges (Medicare definition)—within the context of Medicare Part B, this is the basis of payment for medical services and certain other health services; the reasonable charge is the lowest of either the actual charge billed by the physician or supplier, the charge the physician or supplier customarily bills his patients for the same service, or the prevailing charge most physicians or suppliers in that locality bill for the same service

redisclosure—the disclosure by a third-party recipient, such as a health insurance company, of disclosed health information without the authorization of the patient

redundant array of inexpensive (independent) disks—*see RAID*

registry—Windows NT database that contains hardware, software, OLE, file association, and user and security information required for the operation of Windows 95 and Windows NT

reimbursable costs—allowable costs are determined according to a formula negotiated by the hospital and HMO; the HMO then reimburses the hospital retrospectively, based on the costs incurred according to the agreed upon formula

relational data model—a logical database; it can relate data stored in one table to data in another as long as the two tables share a common data element such as 'name'

release of information—the disclosure of documents containing patient-identifiable information to a third-party requestor such as an insurance company

reliability—a measure of consistency of data based on their consistency, reproducibility and an estimation of their accuracy measurement

reloadable smart card—a smart card containing a microchip that can be used more than one time by reloading the chip with specified amounts of funds

remote access server—*see RAS*

remote access software—the software that enables remote or mobile users to dial into a network and access the network resources

remoteboot—Windows NT network service that can boot MS-DOS and Windows 95 computers from across the network

remote monitoring—a system permitting monitoring of an individual (or a patient) from a different geographical location

remote network monitor—*see RMON*

rendering—process of formatting a print job by the print processor in Windows NT before delivery to a print device

repeater—a device that extends a LAN by increasing the signal of a LAN segment and joining it with another; a computer that forwards every packet appearing on one network to another (active hub)

replication—the exact duplication of a database on two or more nodes of a distributed database system; periodic push duplication of specific data over the network from one server (export) to another (import)

repudiation—denial by one of the persons involved in a communication of having participated in all or part of the communication

RFP—request for proposal; a step during the stage of information system preimplementation that involves an outline of the detailed goals and objectives of the system design, and serves as the communication vehicle for contractors/vendors to return a bid for the system's costs, and to further outline their capabilities to provide the product or services

request for proposal—*see RFP*

resident virus—installs itself as part of the operating system to infect all suitable hosts that are accessed

resolution—measure of graphical image dot density sharpness on a monitor; the higher the density, the sharper the display; common resolutions: 640 X 480, 800 X 600, 1024 X 768, 1280 X 1024

retention—the maintenance and preservation of information in some form (e.g., paper, microfilm, or electronic storage) for a given period of time; there are no federal laws regarding the retention of health information; many states have specific requirements and these, as well as the statutes of limitation, Medicare Conditions of Participation, and use for patient care, legal, research, or educational purposes, are used as a basis for developing retention policies

retro add—retroactive additions to a capitation list; for example, when a member became effectively added for insurance coverage on January 1, but does not appear on the capitation list until April 1, at which point the error is noticed, the member months for this member will require a retro add of three months and a correction of payment

retro delete—retroactive deletions to a capitation list; for example, when a member terminates health plan coverage on January 1, but continues to appear on the capitation list until April 1, at which point the error is noticed, the plan must perform a retro delete of three member months and issue a correction of payment

Reverse Address Resolution Protocol—*see RARP*

reverse engineering—the process of manually, or through the use of expert systems of software tools, extracting the original legacy software design information from source code; *see also legacy system*

RG-8 A/U—.72 mm, 75-ohm coaxial cable used with thick Ethernet 10Base5

RG-11 A/U—.44 mm, 75-ohm coaxial cable used with thick Ethernet 10Base5

RG-58 A/U—.18 mm, 50-ohm coaxial cable used with thin Ethernet 10Base2

RG-59—.58 mm, 75-ohm coaxial cable used with cable TV

RG-62—.64 mm, 93-ohm coaxial cable used with Arcnet

RHIN—regional health information network

right to confidentiality—a patient's right to determine who should have access to the data in his or her records even though the physical record may be owned by someone else (such as a physician or hospital) and even though the information may have been generated by someone other than the patient

right-to-know—specification as to who shall have access to specified data, and the claim by society at large to data with public benefit such as communicable disease data

ring network—network topology in which all computers are linked by a closed loop in a manner that passes data in one direction from one attached computer to another to form a ring in which data packets travel

RIP—routing information protocol; used to advertise and exchange information between routers within an autonomous system

RISC—reduced instruction set computer; nonmicrocode computer that uses a simplified set of instructions in internal firmware to speed operation; Digital Alpha, IBM Power PC, and MIPS are RISC computers

risk analysis—a part of risk management that is used to minimize risk by conducting an assessment of risk and applying security measures commensurate with the relative threats, vulnerabilities, and values of the resources to be protected; the value of the resources includes the impact of the loss or unauthorized modification of data; risk analysis consists of (1) sensitivity assessment, (2) risk assessment, (3) economic assessment, and (4) security test and evaluation

risk assessment in system development—a continuous process performed during all phases of system development to provide an estimate of the damage, loss, or harm that could result from a failure to successfully develop individual components of the system

risk management—the process to identify, control, and minimize the impact of uncertain events; the objective of a risk management program is to reduce risk

RJ-11—six-wire (three-pair) modular plug and jack for use with telephones, modems, and video terminals

RJ-45—eight-wire (four-pair) modular plug and jack for computer network connectivity; used extensively on Ethernet networks with UTP cabling

RMON—remote network monitor; device that collects network traffic information for use by remote monitoring stations

ROM—read only memory; nonvolatile permanent memory written in firmware; contents usually cannot be changed

root directory—system base directory; all other directories and files are found under the root directory

router—a connection or gateway between two computer networks that examines data packets and determines which network to send them to next; device that attaches multiple networks, LANs, and WANs and routes packets between the networks through the use of software; used for communications between networks and operates at the network layer of the OSI model; *see also routing switch and brouter*

routing information protocol—*see RIP*

routing switch—device that attaches multiple networks, LANs, and WANs and routes packets between the networks through the use of hardware; 10 times faster than a conventional router

routing table—lists maintained by routers that include the most recent information on routes advertised by other routers for different destinations

RS-232—slow-speed standard for serial communications between devices; misidentified as RS-232, actually RS-232C

RSA—a public key cryptosystem, invented and patented by Ronald Rivest, Ade Shamir, and Leonard Adelman, based on large prime numbers; RSA is the most well-known asymmetric algorithm

RTS—request to send; modem control operation from DTE requesting clearance to transmit

rule-based expert system—*see expert system*

S/MIME—secure MIME; an extension of the MIME standard to permit encrypted e-mail

S-HTTP—secure HTTP; a system for signing and encrypting information sent over the Web's HTTP protocol; *see HTTP*

sabotage—damage to another person's property, such as computer systems, on purpose

safeguard—a protective measure to mitigate against the effect of system vulnerabilities

safety—the property that a system will satisfy certain criteria related to the preservation of personal and collective freedom from risk

salami—through use of what is called the salami technique, criminals steal resources a little at a time; programs may adjust payroll deductions by just a few cents in each transaction and then collect the funds; this type of transaction is very difficult to detect

sanitization—erasing all identifiers from certain files (i.e., clinical files)

SATAN—security administrator tool for analyzing networks

scanner—a device used to digitize a picture of a document so that it can be stored in memory and on a disk; fax machines use this process to transmit documents to other fax machines

scavenging—the search through discarded materials for pieces of valuable information, especially things like logon IDs and passwords

scheduler—portion of the operating system that moves programs from input to ready

schmeist head—person who executes a system command without knowing what the command will do

SCSI—small computer system interface; high-speed interface for connecting devices to the computer bus; achieves 8-bit data transfer at 5 MB; pronounced "scuzzy"

SCSI-2—small computer system interface-2; high-speed interface for connecting devices to the computer bus; achieves 8-, 16-, or 32-bit data transfer at <10 MB; pronounced "scuzzy"

SCUI—smart card user interface

search engine—a software application that seeks information on the Internet or various designed web servers, based on criteria established by the requesting user

second-level T-Carrier digital trunk—*see T-2*

secondary coverage—refers to the plan or policy that must pay for any medical care or services which the primary payer is not required to reimburse; any insurance (such as privately purchased Medigap, Medicaid, or employer coverage) that supplements Medicare; Medicare is the secondary payer when the beneficiary has other primary insurance, or when reimbursement will be obtained from third-party liability

secondary record—a record that is derived from the primary record and contains only selected data elements

secondary storage—additional storage that is separate from the central processing unit and main memory of data and programs

secondary users of health care information—educational institutions, legal systems, pharmacies, insurance companies, welfare agencies, credit/banking institutions, and public health and research agencies/institutions

secrecy—the intentional concealment or withholding of information

secret key—a key in a symmetric algorithm; the possession of this key is restricted, usually to two persons or organizations

secure electronic transaction—a cryptographic protocol designed for sending encrypted credit card numbers over the Internet

secure socket layer—*see SSL*

secure web server—a program that implements certain crypto-graphic protocols so that it is not possible to eavesdrop on information transferred between a web server and a web browser; a server resistant to an attack over the Internet or from institutional insiders

security—control of access and protection of information from accidental or intentional disclosure to any unauthorized persons and from alteration, destruction, or loss; protection of information systems against unauthorized access to or modification of information, whether in storage, processing, or transit, and against the denial of service to authorized users or the provision of service to unauthorized users, including those measures necessary to detect, document, and counter such threats

security administrator—a member of the system management team trained in data security matters, authorized to enforce those measures and to create a confidentiality/privacy-conscious working environment

security administration control—all management control measures and appropriate policies necessary to provide an acceptable level of protection of data stored in the data system

security compromise—a specific loss of information or data due to an unauthorized person obtaining secured files

security, designed-in—the provision of hardware and software features to ensure security from the inception and design of the system

security education program—systematic method to provide information and to teach skills related to all activities of an organization related to information security; a complete information security education program addresses policies, standards, training, controls, risk assessment, auditing and monitoring, and assigned responsibility for management of the program

security level—security level is categorization of controlled resources or specified data users

security manager—the person assigned responsibility for management of an organization's security program; focal point for the overall coordination of security policy and procedures for an organization

security overhead—the total cost of the added hardware features and software required to serve safeguarding purposes

security policy—the framework in an organization that establishes needed levels of information security to achieve confidentiality goals; a statement of information values, protection responsibilities, and organization commitment for a system; it is a set of laws, rules, and practices that regulate how an organization manages, protects, and distributes sensitive information; it is recommended that security policies must apply to all employees, medical staff members, volunteers, students, faculty, independent contractors, and agents

security system of a data system—the integrated combination of technology, security administrator's activities, and honoring the related statutory laws which is intended to prevent accidental or unauthorized disclosure of data, modification or destruction of stored data, or damage to the data system, and reduce risk to an acceptable level

security tool—a program run to evaluate or enhance the security of a system

security threats, authorizer—incorrect or inaccurate specification of authorizations

security threats, categories—*see security threats, authorizer; security threats, data security person; security threats, physical environment; security threats, technical failures; security threats, user*

security threats, data security person—inadequate security supervision, insufficient monitoring of operations, inadequate control of personnel

security threats, physical environment—natural disasters such as water, fire, electricity failure, earthquake, or malicious attacks

security threats, technical failures—hardware: failure of protection safeguard mechanisms; software: loopholes, incorrect use of protective software, failure of software safeguards, system crash; operator: duplication of data; initializing an insecure state; disabling or disarming of the security system

security threats, user—fraudulent identification; accessing unauthorized data; releasing data to secondary users, who are unauthorized access; altering accessed data

semantics—the associated meaning of a set of symbols within a given language

sendmail—a common type of electronic mail used over the Internet; an attacker can install malicious code in an electronic mail message and mail to a networked machine; sendmail scans the message looking for the address, then executes the attacker's code

sensitivity label—a security level associated with the content of the information; information that is considered to have a heightened potential for causing harm to a patient, or to others, such as the subject's spouse, children, friends, or sexual partners; the degree to which information will cause humiliation, stigmatization, lost employment, insurance problems, or loss of family and friends all contributes to it being identified as "sensitive"

sequenced packet exchange—*see SPX*

Serial Line IP—*see SLIP*

server—centralized network computer that provides an array of resources and services to network users

server software—a program that responds to a request from a client

services for the Macintosh—*see SFM*

session layer—fifth layer of the OSI model; provides file management needed to support intersystem communication through the use of synchronization and data stream checkpoints; also responsible for the establishment, management, and termination of sessions; when a workstation logs on to a server, the server's session layer determines what the workstation's access permissions are, and serves as a coordinator for interactions between programs on different nodes

SET—*see secure electronic transaction*

set computer—*see RISC*

SFM—services for the Macintosh; provides file and print services for Macintosh computers on a Windows NT network via the AppleTalk protocol

Sfmmon.dll—Windows NT print monitor for print jobs delivered to Apple/MAC-based printers

SGML—Standard General Mark-up Language; this language is used as the basis for Hypertext Markup Language (HTML) and is used in the printing of coded documents; *see also HTML*

shielded twisted pair—*see STP*

SIG—special interest group; subset of professional computer organizations that concentrates on a specific technical computing area

SIMM—single in-line memory module; a type of RAM chip

Simple Mail Transfer Protocol—*see SMTP*

Simple Network Monitoring Protocol—*see SNMP*

simplex—communication channel/circuit that allows data transmission in one direction only

simulation—a modeling technique using statistical, rather than analytical, relationships between variables to model a solvable problem

simultaneous peripheral operation on-line—*see SPOOLING*

single domain—Windows NT single network domain without trusts to other domains; best suited for small networks with centralized administration of accounts and resources

single in-line memory module—*see SIMM*

single master domain—Windows NT master network domain with a single administration domain for accounts and trusts to resource domains administered by those domains

SLIP—Serial Line Internet Protocol; minimal overhead protocol for TCP/IP only data transfer over serial links; does not support multiple protocols, encryption, or compression; a precursor to Point-to-Point Protocol; *see also PPP*

small computer system interface—*see SCSI*

small computer system interface-2—*see SCSI-2*

smart card—a credit card-like device that contains an integrated circuit chip or microprocessor to store, process, and exchange data or information with a computer system; it is called "smart" because of the IC chip; it can also be used as an access control device, carrying security functions to maintain a more secure and efficient access control for computer systems

smart card operating system—organizes data on the integrated circuit chip into files and protects them from unauthorized access

smart card user interface—provides a standard interface between applications and the data on the chip; multiple applications can reside on the chip, and the SCUI allows an application to access its own data without affecting another application's data

SMAU—multiple station access unit; token-ring network hub

SMTP—Simple Mail Transfer Protocol; protocol used to transfer mail between systems

SNA—System Network Architecture; network architecture developed by IBM for mainframe networking; does not interoperate with TCP/IP

sniffer—network tool that collects network traffic packets to provide analysis on network and protocol usage and generates statistics to assist in monitoring and optimizing networks; identifies bottlenecks, traffic, and utilization patterns; also known as a protocol analyzer or network analyzer; programs used to intercept clear text data in packets transmitted through local area networks; a method of eavesdropping on communications

SNMP—Simple Network Monitoring Protocol; used to monitor hosts, routers, and networks; enables a monitoring management station to configure, monitor, and receive alarms from network devices

SNOMED—Systematized Nomenclature of Medicine

soft copy—file maintained on disk in electronic storage format

software—the program used to direct the functions of a computer system

software access—the ability and the means to communicate with the operating system or any file/database controlled by the operating system of a clinical data system

software maintenance—any work performed on a software system after it enters implementation

software reengineering—converting an aging software application into a modern, well-structured application, often using a new coding language and/or database, and supported by reengineering tools

software security system—a computer operating system certified to contain those hardware and software functions and features required to prohibit an accidental or malicious access

solid state floppy disk card (SSFDC)—a smart card configuration using a NAND Flash EEPROM memory chip, primarily supplied by Toshiba; it is shaped like a miniaturized floppy disk and is the same thickness as a credit card, but one-third the size; capacity of 8 MB; the SSFDC is installed in many digital cameras and game devices

SONET—Synchronous Optical Network; ANSI standard for high-speed, high-quality digital optical transmission

special interest group—*see SIG*

SPIN—standard prescriber identification number; a unique identifier that was proposed for future use to support prescribing providers in an effort to be headed by the National Council of Prescription Drug Programs and other professional organizations; *see also NPI*

spooler—service that buffers data for low-speed output devices; uses disks as buffers for data storage until an output device is ready

SPOOLING—simultaneous peripheral operation on-line; *see spooler*

spreadsheet—a software application with an electronic table of rows and columns that provides a quick method for performance of mathematical calculations, or tabulations

SPX—sequenced packet exchange; connection-oriented portion of the NetWare IPX/SPX protocol package

SSFDC—*see solid state floppy disk card*

SSH—secure shell; encrypted remote terminal that provides confidentiality and authentication

SSL—secure socket layer; secure method of data transfer between a web browser and a web server; a system that automatically encrypts information as it is sent over the Internet and decrypts it before it is used

stack—LIFO data holding structure; *see also LIFO*

standard Ethernet—*see 10Base5*

standard prescriber identification number—*see also SPIN and NPI*

standard reports—most management information system software contains standard reports, as opposed to customized ad hoc reports, which are generated to assist management in evaluating performance of providers, claims experience, or learning the characteristics of enrolled membership

star network—type of LAN topology where networked nodes are connected to a hub at a central point; the benefits of a star network include the ability to easily add or remove elements of the network, such as a workstation

star topology—*see star network*

static audit tool—system scanner to look for and report weaknesses

static memory—memory that does not need to be refreshed while power is maintained; faster than dynamic memory

stealth virus—a type of virus that attempts to evade detection by concealing its presence in infected files; to achieve this, the virus removes all signs of its presence

steganography—hiding information in routine files and documents; e.g., insertion of instructions that modify portions of a program's output to carry information; used to steal information

stored value card—a smart card with a microchip that is used to carry funds and is used for purchases

stove-pipe system—*see closed system and also open systems architecture*

STP—shielded twisted pair; 1.5-inch diameter type of cabling where the wire pairs are twisted together in a shielded protective jacket to reduce the effects of EMI; used to implement 10BaseT and 100BaseT networks

stream algorithms—encrypt data byte by byte

subnet mask—32-bit portion of an IP address that identifies a specific network or host within a subnetwork

substitution—a method of cryptography based on the principle of replacing each letter in the message with another one

substitution cipher—in encryption programs, a substitution cipher replaces the characters of the original plain text message; the characters retain their original position, but are altered

super video graphics array—*see SVGA*

superzapping—the unauthorized use of utility computer programs that modify, copy, disclose, destroy, insert, use, or deny use of data stored in a computer or on computer media; a type of computer crime

surge protector—*see surge suppressor*

surge suppressor—a device to protect systems against power spikes

SVGA—super video graphics array; color display system providing high-resolution graphics displays of multiple colors at various resolutions

SVGD—super video graphic display

switch—high-throughput network communications OSI layer two device that directs packets to specific nodes

switched networks—a type of system in which each user has a unique address that allows the network to directly connect any two points

symmetric key algorithms—encryption algorithm in which the same key is used to encrypt and decrypt a message

symmetric multiprocessing—multiprocessing technique that utilizes all available processors in a computer to execute the operating system and applications

Synchronous Optical NETwork—*see SONET*

synchronous transmission—high-speed simultaneous transmission of large blocks of data into timed intervals, between computers or terminals within a network

system—a set of interrelated parts that function together as a whole towards a common purpose

System Network Architecture—*see SNA*

system security—the result of all safeguards of hardware, software, personnel policies, information practice policies, disaster preparedness, and their oversight

system security administrator—the person who controls access to computer systems, assigning user access codes and privileges, revoking user access privileges, and setting file protection parameters

system test—a test to determine that the results generated by the entire enterprise information system and its components are accurate and that the system performs to specification; *see also user test and unit test*

T-1—first-level T-Carrier digital trunk; 1.544 Mbps bandwidth available line using one T-1 channel; a T-1 is the most common communications point-to-point (PPP) full duplex transmission line between networks; *see also full duplex and PPP*

T-2—second-level T-Carrier digital trunk; 6.312 Mbps bandwidth available using four T-1 channels; provides four times the bandwidth of a T-1

T-3—third-level T-Carrier digital trunk; 44.736 Mbps bandwidth available using 28 T-1 channels; used as a synonym for DS3

T-4—fourth-level T-Carrier digital trunk; 274.176 Mbps bandwidth available using 168 T-1 channels

T-568A—the connection instructions or punchdown assignments for RJ-45 modular wall jacks sequenced as

Pin Color	Name
1 white/green	Rcv Data +
2 green	Rcv Data –
3 white/orange	
4 blue	
5 white/blue	
6 orange	TxData–
7 white/brown	
8 brown	

T-568B—the connection instructions or punchdown assignments for RJ-45 modular wall jacks sequenced as

Pin Color	Name
1 white/orange	TxData +
2 orange	TxData–
3 white/green	RevData+
4 blue	
5 white/blue	
6 green	RevData–
7 white/brown	
8 brown	

table—a graphical format for data with unique names or values, depicted in a matrix-type structure of columns and rows

Taligent—the company formed by Apple and IBM to develop an object-oriented operating system named Pink

tampering—unauthorized modification that alters the proper functioning of a smart card

task manager—Windows NT 4.0 utility that presents application, process, and performance information; displays the status of all executing applications; shows the status of all active processes; provides information on CPU usage, memory usage, and physical memory statistics

T-Carrier—high-speed, point-to-point full duplex communications line identified in different levels: T1, T2, T3, and T4

TCP—Transmission Control Protocol; connection-oriented data transmission mode portion of TCP/IP; protocol for sending information in streams of data; reference model used for linking different types of computers and networks

TCP/IP—Transmission Control Protocol/Internet Protocol; routable protocol required for Internet accesses; the TCP portion is associated with data; IP is associated with source-to-destination packet delivery

TDR—time-domain reflectometer; testing device that sends sound waves along cabling to detect shorts or breaks in the cable

technical specification—a technical description of the desired functionality of a system, as derived from its requirements; a specification is used to develop and test an implementation of a system

telecommunications—use of wire, radio, optical, or other electromagnetic channels to transmit or receive signals for voice, data, and video communications

Telecommunications Network—*see Telnet*

teleconferencing—inactive electronic communications between two or more people at two or more sites, which makes use of voice, video, and/or data transmission systems

teleconsulting—use of communications technology to overcome geographic separation between two or more providers during a consultation

teledermatology—a technology allowing images of the skin to be transmitted via a modem from the patient to a consulting dermatologist in another location

telehealth—use of advanced telecommunications technologies to exchange health information and provide health care services across geographic, time, social, and cultural barriers; this may allow faster diffusion and extension of Health Decision Support System (HDSS) technology through increased communication capabilities in a wider pool of communicators; *see also HDSS*

tele-imaging—electronic transmission of images from one locale to another for interpretation and/or consultation

telemedicine—the ability to use centralized medical expertise to provide care to patients in rural areas, and for centralized physicians to speak and share images with rural doctors through two-way visual and audio networks that allow an electronic house-call; telemedicine, such as teleradiology, precludes the rural patient's need for transportation to an urban area to receive care, and reduces other staff or equipment costs in rural areas, servicing nearly a third of today's rural hospitals

telemonitoring—use of audio, video, and other telecommunications and electronic information processing technologies to monitor patient status from a distance

telephone follow-up—*see patient telemanagement*

telephone hotline, or physician directory—*see physician referral service*

telephone triage system—a demand management or customer-oriented tool that allows patients to call by telephone to relate their problems or medical symptoms; by use of preapproved medical protocols, the triage operator is able to give advice, prescribe home remedies, or determine whether the patient should be seen within a given time period; telephone triage systems have achieved positive results by precluding unnecessary visits to the emergency room, or to a doctors office—most current systems are designed to err on the side of inviting the patient to be seen (or calling a physician directly) rather than to risk missing a genuine medical problem; for-profit companies offer standard protocol for sale to providers, which are often backed up by telephone recording devices to record conversations for possible review later; also may be called nurse hotline, nurse triage system, pediatric hotline

telepresence—use of robotics and other technology that allow a person (e.g., a surgeon) to perform a task at a remote site by manipulating instruments (e.g., lasers or dental handpieces) and receiving sensory information or feed (e.g., pressure like that created by touching a patient) that creates a sense of being present to the remote site and allows a satisfactory degree of technical performance

telepsychiatry—use of telehealth technology to connect the patient to the psychiatrist to allow diagnosis, education, and treatment across barriers of geography, time, and culture

teleradiology—this concept and evolving area of medical information systems includes the use of telehealth technology for radiological practices and innovations; initial image capture may be digitized, retrieved with varying degrees of compression, reviewed remotely, or forwarded to remote locations by telecommunications pathways

telerobotic surgery—the practice of remote surgery, using robotic arms to wield and manipulate surgical tools, such as scalpels, clamps, and needles; *see also telepresence*

Telnet—derived from telecommunications network; protocol for remote terminal service connectivity; connectivity from one site to interact with a remote system

terabyte—approximately one trillion bytes; unit of computer storage capacity

terminal printing suppression—suppressing the printing of passwords or other access control information; used to thwart unauthorized access to a computer system

terminal server—network communications device that allows one or more serial devices to connect to an Ethernet LAN; used extensively throughout CHCS with the LAT protocol

test facility—a computer system isolated from the day-to-day production environment, for the purpose of testing and validating the compatibility of various applications or system components

TFTP—Trivial File Transfer Protocol; minimal overhead file transfer used to upload or download bootstrap files to diskless workstations through the use of UDP

thicknet—*see 10Base5*

thinnet—*see 10Base2*

third-level T-Carrier digital trunk—*see T-3*

third-party administrator—*see TPA*

third-party liability—exists if an entity is liable to pay the medical cost for injury, disease, or disability of a person hurt during the performance of his or her occupation, and the injury is caused by an entity not connected with the employer; an increasingly significant consideration for recouping payment from over 20 possible sources that have been outlined in terms of sequential responsibility to pay by various state and federal laws, and the National Association of Insurance Commissioners (NAIC), beginning with the patient and extending through various group plan criteria, other individual and family insurance, Medicare, Medicare supplements, Program for the Handicapped, Civilian Health and Medical Program of the Uniformed Services/Veterans Adminsitration (CHAMPUS/VA) or Maternal and Child Health or Indian Health Service, CHAMPUS supplements, and lastly, Medicaid

third-party payer—a public or private organization that pays for or underwrites coverage for health care expenses or another entity, usually an employer, such as Blue Cross and Blue Shield, Medicare, Medicaid, or commercial insurers; also called third-party carrier; the individual enrollee generally pays a premium for coverage in all private and some public programs, then the organization pays bills on the patient's behalf, which are called third-party payments

third-party payment—the third party is a payer or carrier that makes payment to a provider (the second party) on behalf of the patient (the first party)

thread—the smallest portion handled by the processor's scheduler

threat—the potential for exploitation of a vulnerability; *see accidental threat, active threat, deliberate threat, logical threat, passive threat*

throughput—amount of information that a medium delivers in a given time to determine performance

thunking—translation that takes place from 32-bit to 16-bit code

time bomb—a type of logic bomb that "explodes" at a certain time, such as a certain date; can be used to damage disk directories on a certain date

time-domain reflectometer—*see TDR*

time to live—*see TTL*

token—a physical device necessary for user identification that is used in the context of authentication

token bus network—type of LAN topology where networked nodes are connected to the main cable of the network and which uses a token for transmission access; *see IEEE 802.4*

token ring—packet used for LAN access in a token-based network; the node that possesses the token, controls the transmission medium and is allowed to transmit on the network; it guarantees that a computer can transmit at regular intervals, and other computers must wait for a free token to transmit data

token ring network—type of LAN topology where networked nodes are connected at points to form a ring in which data packets travel; uses a token for transmission access; *see IEEE 802.5*

topology—physical layout or architecture of a network; bus, star, ring, and hybrid are network topologies

touch screen—input technology that permits the entering or selecting of commands and data by touching the surface of a sensitized video display monitor with a finger or pointer

TPA—third-party administrator; any third party entity which administers health plan entitlements and is supported by the infrastructure to process claims; a TPA does not underwrite the risk of a contract, but performs largely administrative functions that are supported by computer systems; as markets mature, many TPAs are looking to evolve into other lines of business, since HMOs and providers are becoming more able to perform the TPA primary mission

traceroute—program that provides source-to-destination path router information; the route which packets are following to reach a particular node

transmission—the exchange of data between a person and a program, or a program and a program, when the sender and receiver are remote from each other

Transmission Control Protocol—*see TCP*

Transmission Control Protocol/Internet Protocol—*see TCP/IP*

transport layer—fourth layer of the OSI model; handles the interface between hardware levels and software levels; provides for end-to-end flow control and ensures that messages are delivered error-free; the transport layer ensures data are successfully sent by verifying the network layer's data for errors and requesting retransmission of the data when necessary, and it looks for alternative routes or saves data until the connection has been re-established; *see also network layer*

transposition—a method of cryptography based on the principle of scrambling the characters in a message

transposition cipher—a transposition cipher in cryptography rearranges the characters of the original plain text message, rendering the characters unchanged but altering their position, making the text unintelligible

trap doors—a way that an unauthorized user gains access to hardware or software that would normally not be available;

may be the result of knowledge of features that should be available only to a few persons

Trivial File Transfer Protocol—*see TFTP*

Trojan horse—a program that appears to have one universal function, but actually has a hidden malicious function; a program that performs a known task, but also includes unexpected and usually undesirable functions; does not replicate

trunk—single circuit between two switching center points; handles many channels simultaneously

trust—Windows NT domain association with another Windows NT domain where the domains trust each other with resources

trusted system—a system assured to perform a given set of attributes to a stated degree of assurance or confidence

trusted-user access level—a system user who needs access to sensitive information

TTL—time to live; length of active Internet time technique used to avoid endlessly looped packets; every packet is assigned a decrementing TTL; packets with expired TTLs are discarded by routers

twisted-pair cable—cable consisting of copper core wires surrounded by an insulator; a pair, consisting of two wires twisted together, forms a circuit that can transmit data; the twisting helps to prevent interference

Type 1 IBM Token Ring Cabling—shielded twisted pair (STP)

Type 2 IBM Token Ring Cabling—combination of UTP and STP

Type 3 IBM Token Ring Cabling—four-pair UTP; *see also UTP*

Type 5 IBM Token Ring Cabling—fiber-optic main ring

Type 6 IBM Token Ring Cabling—same as type 1 and type 2 but used to cover shorter distances

Type 8 IBM Token Ring Cabling—used for under-carpet runs

Type 9 IBM Token Ring Cabling—fire retardant cabling, used to support token ring topology

UART—universal asynchronous receiver transmitter; motherboard component that converts serial data to parallel data and vice versa

UDK—user-defined keys; used to store frequently used commands through the F6 to F20 keys on a video terminal keyboard

UDP—user datagram protocol; connectionless transmission protocol; protocol for sending information as a series of packets

UM—utilization management; the process of evaluating the necessity, appropriateness, and efficiency of health care services; a review coordinator or medical director gathers information about the proposed hospitalization, service, or procedure from the patient and/or provider, then determines whether it meets established guidelines and criteria, which may be written or automated protocols approved by the organization; a provider or Integrated Delivery Network that proves it is skilled in UM may negotiate more advantageous pricing if UM is normally performed by the HMO but could be more effectively passed downward to a provider at a savings to the HMO

UMLS—Unified Medical Language System

UNC—Universal Naming Convention; text-based method to identify the path to a remote device, server, directory, or file; implemented as: \\computername\sharename\directoryname\ filename

uniform hospital discharge data set—a list of data elements and their associated definitions that comprise the minimum set to be collected on discharged hospital patients

uniform resource locator—*see URL*

uninterruptible power supply—*see UPS*

unit numbering—a scheme for numbering patients within a facility, in which only one number is permanently assigned to a patient for record-tracking purposes

unit record—a single record location for all associated documents or records of a health patient

unit test—other types of tests include user test to determine if user requirements are satisfied, and unit tests to determine if individual components perform

universal asynchronous receiver transmitter—*see UART*

universal identifier—a means to provide definite recognition of a particular individual; a universal health care or patient identifier provides the identifier for use in health care transactions

Universal Naming Convention—*see UNC*

UNIX—operating system for microcomputers, minicomputers, and mainframes that is machine-independent and supports multi-user processing, multitasking, and networking

UNIX System V—standard UNIX operating system; multitasking operating system developed in the early 1970s

unshielded twisted pair—*see UTP; see also CAT-1, CAT-2, CAT-3, CAT-4, and CAT-5*

UPS—uninterruptible power supply; device that keeps a computer running by maintaining constant power via battery; provides the opportunity for a graceful shutdown in a commercial power-out condition; a device used to protect against a loss or insufficient amount of power by providing a stable amount of power during a period of time specified by the type and price range of the device

UR—utilization review; the evaluation of medical necessity and efficiency or quality of health care services, either prospectively, concurrently, or retrospectively; contrasted with utilization management in that UR is more limited to the physician's diagnosis, treatment, and billing amount, whereas UM addresses the wider program requirements; *see also UM*

URL—uniform resource locator; provides the unique location information by using a naming convention of protocol type followed by a specific service, such as "http//:ibm.com" or "ftp//:ibm.com/files"; this address mechanism for the Internet allows the user to "surf" or connect to network resource sites, by identifying the URL and connecting to that web site; *see also HTML*

UR/UM—utilization review/utilization management; these features or modules within a health care information system must handle a variety of: each authorization or referral—by provider, protocol, or benefit level; utilization and rate for each contracted entity, provider, and type of treatment; and the patterns of treatment by provider

user—person presenting a smart card for a transaction or process

user access—a person or an organization authorized to access data for legitimate purposes such as teaching or research

user access level—the level to which a user is allowed to access data or computer files; often dependent upon job requirements

user authentication—the provision of assurance of the claimed identity of an individual or entity

user-defined keys—*see UDK*

user interface—the part of an information system through which a user interacts with the system; type of hardware and the series of on-screen commands and responses required for a user to interact with a system

user test—the portion of the testing phases that are used to determine if all user requirements are satisfied, and that the system performs according to user-defined requirements; *see also system test and unit test*

utility program—system software consisting of programs for routine, repetitive tasks, which are shared by several users

utilization—the use of health care services and supplies by an enrolled member or a group, which has become the focus of the managed care discipline, to ensure the medical necessity and appropriateness of all expenses; typically measured in areas of admissions per thousand patients enrolled, visits per thousand, hospital bed days per thousand, etc.; *see also UM*

utilization care plan—a standardized patient care management template created on the basis of case-mix groupings that can reside in a computer database to support comprehensive and high-quality patient care

utilization review/utilization management—*see UR/UM*

UTP—unshielded twisted pair; type of cabling where the insulated wire conductors are twisted together in an unshielded voice-grade cable; used to implement 10BaseT and 100BaseT networks

V codes—a classification of ICD-9-CM coding to identify health care encounters for reasons other than illness or injury and to identify patients whose injury or illness is influenced by special circumstances or problems

validation—the process of evaluating a system or component during or at the end of the development process to determine whether it satisfies specified requirements

validity—the extent to which data correspond to the actual state of affairs, or the extent to which an instrument is able to measure what is stated it will measure

VAN—value added network; a specialized common carrier that "adds value" above the standard level of service

value added network—*see VAN*

vaporware—software that does not currently exist but may be introduced sometime in the future

variant virus—a type of virus generated by modifying a known virus; the modifications may add functionality, or ways to evade detection

VDM—virtual DOS machine; Windows NT protected memory implementation for the execution of DOS-16 and Win16 applications

very high-level language—*see VHLL*

VGA—video graphics array; color display system providing high-resolution graphics displays of 16 colors at a 640 x 480 resolution and 256 colors at a 320 x 200 resolution

VHLL—very high-level language; part of an end-user tool that allows programming individuals, with only limited knowledge of computers, the ability to develop their own applications

video graphics array—see VGA

video teleconferencing—*see VTC*

virtual card—the data elements contained in the data indices without regard for physical addresses

virtual community-based health care system—a health care system where information and knowledge are accessible and affordable (e.g., through the Internet); one goal of the system is to empower the consumers and increase their role in making decisions that affect their health and well-being

virtual DOS machine—*see VDM*

virtual Internet applications—applications that are provided from the Internet and are accessed through a computer; examples can include news, journals, references, consumer-oriented information to educate users on health issues, or actual medical applications on the Internet

virtual reality—a computer-based technology for stimulating visual, auditory, and other sensory aspects of complex environments by making the user feel that he or she is experiencing a segment of real life

virtual real-time—accessibility without the impeded geographical distance and time-zone differences combined with real-time processing; virtual real-time processing allows a virtual organization to provide efficient and coordinated service

virus—a malicious computer program that makes copies of itself and attaches those copies to other programs and changes them; *see variant virus; overwriting virus; nonoverwriting virus; resident virus; stealth virus*

Visual Basic—a Microsoft product that is an advanced and modular programming language with user-friendly, screen-driven programming that may include subroutines

VMS—Virtual Memory System

voice mail—telephone messaging that uses computerized features to record, replay, forward, or process messages that are left by incoming telephone callers

voice recognition—a natural language interface where commands are sent vocally without the use of the keyboard

voice response system—a unit that allows a customer to call in by telephone, and give instructions to a computer by speaking or by pressing digits on the phone; the input may be used in multiple health care applications to reduce costs, direct the caller to the appropriate office without use of an operator, and avoid other shortfalls of speaking with staff during certain limited business hours, such as pharmacy refill call-in systems, telephone appointments, or HMO member services customer support; may be part of an overall integrated call management system, to include call screen transfer capability

VTC—video teleconferencing; a real-time communication between two or more parties, using transmissions of digitized video images between two or more locations

vulnerability—a weakness in a system that can be used to violate a system's intended behavior; there may be security, integrity, availability, and other vulnerabilities; the act of exploiting a vulnerability represents a threat, which has an associated risk of being exploited

vulnerable user access level—the level to which a user is allowed to access data or computer files; is often dependent upon job requirements

WAN—wide area network; a network in which the computers are connected by various configurations of telecommunications lines and intermediate hardware devices, but may be separated by considerable distances; used to describe a network that extends beyond a local area network (LAN); *see also LAN*

WARP—IBM's OS/2 Version 4.0 32-bit GUI multitasking operating system with the ability to run DOS, Win16, Win32, OS/2 16, and OS/2 32 applications for 80486 and Pentium computers

waterfall method or model—a first-generation systems development process that embodies the systems development life-cycle concept and consists of six steps: feasibility study, systems investigation, systems analysis, systems design, systems implementation, and systems maintenance and review

wavelet—a software compression algorithm, such as that used with radiological studies

WBS—work breakdown structure; used in contracting or project management to divide a job into smaller objectives, activities, and subactivities that are required to complete the work

web address—*see IP address*

web browser—the PC Client portion of the WWW server access through HTTP; usually a GUI interface; *see also search engine*

web security—a set of protocols and technologies to protect web servers, users, and their organizations

web server—WWW server that displays services through URLs for web browser connectivity; the dedicated computers on which web pages reside, or the program on that computer that receives network requests and transmits web page files in response

web site—an Internet location which generally begins with the first page or home page as an introduction or index to other information within the site; *see also home page*

wide area network—*see WAN*

wide SCSI—wide small computer system interface; 20 Mbps to 40 Mbps high-speed interface for connecting devices to the computer bus; pronounced "scuzzy"

wide small computer system interface—*see Wide SCSI*

Win16—Windows NT subsystem for running 16-bit applications

Win32—Windows NT subsystem for running 32-bit applications

Winchester Drive—hard drive associated with AT computers that employed the MFM recording technique

Windows—Microsoft's graphical operating system; first introduced in 1985

Windows 3.11—Windows for Workgroups; Microsoft's graphical operating system with networking capability

Windows 95—Microsoft's 32-bit graphical multitasking operating system; known as Chicago during development; introduced in 1995

Windows Internetwork Naming Service—*see WINS*

Windows NT Server—Microsoft's 32-bit graphical multitasking and symmetric multiprocessing network operating system

Windows NT Workstation—Microsoft's 32-bit graphical multitasking and symmetric multiprocessing operating system

Windows on Windows—*see WOW and VDM*

WINS—Windows Internetwork Naming Service; a Microsoft database that dynamically maps and maintains a listing of computer (NetBIOS) names to IP addresses on a network

wireless technology—recent radio frequency (RF) architecture that transmits signals from remote, lightweight workstations to the wireless local area network (LAN) in such a way that health-related work processes can be reengineered toward greater mobility with an improved focus on the patient, such as bedside patient registration; *see also LAN*

work breakdown structure—*see WBS*

workstation—a node, intelligent terminal, or computer attached to a network that runs local applications or connects to servers to access shared server resources; usually a microcomputer; *see also dumb terminal*

World Wide Web—*see WWW*

WORM—write once, read many (times); process used for applications where permanent data storage is required; an optical laser disk that can be read many times after the data are written to it; the data cannot be changed or erased

worm—a self-replicating program similar to a virus; it hides its existence and spreads copies of itself within a computer system or through networks

WOW—Windows on Windows; synonymous with VDM

wrapping—FDDI network and fault tolerance process that isolates a problem area within the network; routes transmissions around the problem area through the use of the second FDDI ring

WWW—World Wide Web; *see also Internet*

X.25—packet-switching network protocol with extensive error-checking and accounting capability; employs the use of permanent virtual circuits (PVC), switched virtual circuits (SVC), and packet assemblers and dissemblers; the most popular packet-switching protocol in Europe

XENIX—Microsoft's PC operating system related closely to UNIX; developed in the early 1980s

XNS—Xerox Network System

XOR—exclusive OR; logical gating operation that provides a high output if only one input is high

XT—Extended Technology; IBM PC 8088 CPU series; introduced in 1983

X-Windows—standard graphical windowing system for UNIX machines; developed at MIT to provide a GUI environment for UNIX users via bitmapped displays

Y2K—the calendar year 2000, as it relates to the difficulty of some systems in handling the next century date; a special process to prevent problems involves the inventory of all software, hardware, and network components to ensure that they have the capability to properly handle a four-byte field for the year (such as the ability to differentiate between 1900, 2000, and 2100), versus only having the two-byte field for "00"; after the inventory phase, most programs begin with an assessment phase, followed by the correction of any problems or deficiencies, and finally testing to ensure compliance

Y2K-compliant—an information system's ability to accurately process the date data—including, but not limited to, calculating, comparing, and sequencing information from, into, and between the 20th and 21st Centuries, including leap-year calculations

Y2K problem—the potential problems and their variations that might be encountered in any level of automated hardware, software, or network from microcode to applications programs, files, and databases that need to correctly interpret year-date data represented in a two-digit-year format

Y2K system—any automated process that uses information technology to perform a specific function, application, or service surrounding the Year 2000; *see also Y2K*

Year 2000—*see Y2K*

Z

Zilog Z80—late 1970s IBM 8088 processor with features to execute additional op codes; operated at 25 MHz and used in an array of computing devices

Zombie—a UNIX process that does not terminate, but must be removed by the kill command